**Editor**
Evan D. Forbes, M.S. Ed.

**Editorial Project Manager**
Charles Payne, M.A., M.F.A

**Editor in Chief**
Sharon Coan, M.S. Ed.

**Illustrator**
Larry Bauer

**Photo Cover Credit**
Images provided by
PhotoDisc ©1994

**Art Coordinator**
Denice Adorno

**Creative Director**
Elayne Roberts

**Imaging**
Evan D. Forbes, M.S. Ed.

**Product Manager**
Phil Garcia

**Publishers**
Rachelle Cracchiolo, M.S. Ed.
Mary Dupuy Smith, M.S. Ed.

Teacher Created Materials

Hands-On Minds-On Science

# Ocean

*Primary*

# Table of Contents

# Table of Contents *(cont.)*

# Introduction

**What Is Science?**

What is science to young children? Is it something that they know is a part of their world? Is it a textbook in the classroom? Is it a tadpole changing into a frog? It is a sprouting seed, a rainy day, a boiling pot, a turning wheel, a pretty rock, or a moonlit sky? Is science fun and filled with wonder and meaning? What is science to children?

Science offers you and your eager students opportunities to explore the world around you and make connections between the things you experience. The world becomes your classroom, and you, the teacher, a guide.

Science can, and should, fill children with wonder. It should cause them to be filled with questions and the desire to discover the answers to their questions. And, once they have discovered answers, they should be actively seeking new questions to answer.

The books in this series give you and the students in your classroom the opportunity to learn from the whole of your experience—the sights, sounds, smells, tastes, and touches, as well as what you read, write about, and do. This whole-science approach allows you to experience and understand your world as you explore science concepts and skills together.

**What Is the Ocean?**

When astronauts view the Earth from their orbiting satellites, they see it as a vast blue sphere. Where does all this blue come from? The ocean, that huge body of water which covers more than 2/3 of the globe. Although man has named five different oceans, there is actually only one which is separated by land masses. An astonishing array of plants and animals call the ocean their home. Most of these species cannot survive outside of this watery environment. Their colors and varieties are unequaled anywhere else on earth. Some are as old as the beginning of time. Others are slowly diminishing due to pollution or overharvesting by man. We cannot afford to let our oceans die because we depend on them for so many things—minerals, medicine, food, and fuel, for example. Finally, the ocean plays an important part in the hydrologic cycle. Although ocean water itself is impotable because of its high salt content, its waters are purified as it goes through the water cycle and returns to land in the form of precipitation. Without water, life as we know it would cease to exist. The ocean is truly the foundation of life.

# The Scientific Method

The "scientific method" is one of several creative and systematic processes for proving or disproving a given question, following an observation. When the scientific method is used in the classroom, a basic set of guiding principles and procedures is followed in order to answer a question. However, real world science is often not as rigid as the scientific method would have us believe.

This systematic method of problem solving will be described in the paragraphs that follow.

## 1 Make an OBSERVATION.

The teacher presents a situation, gives a demonstration, or reads background material that interests students and prompts them to ask questions. Or students can make observations and generate questions on their own as they study a topic.

*Example: A display of a variety of seaweeds.*

## 2 Select a QUESTION to investigate.

In order for students to select a question for a scientific investigation, they will have to consider the materials they have or can get, as well as the resources (books, magazines, people, etc.) actually available to them. You can help them make an inventory of their materials and resources, either individually or as a group.

Tell students that in order to successfully investigate the questions they have selected, they must be very clear about what they are asking. Discuss effective questions with your students. Depending upon their level, simplify the question or make it more specific.

*Example: What are some ways in which we eat seaweed?*

## 3 Make a PREDICTION (hypothesis).

Explain to students that a hypothesis is a good guess about what the answer to a question will probably be. But they do not want to make just any arbitrary guess. Encourage students to predict what they think will happen and why.

In order to formulate a hypothesis, students may have to gather more information through research.

Have students practice making hypotheses with questions you give them. Tell them to pretend they have already done their research. You want them to write each hypothesis so it follows these rules:

1. It is to the point.
2. It tells what will happen, based on what the question asks.
3. It follows the subject/verb relationship of the question.

*Example: I think we can find seaweed in different food products.*

# The Scientific Method *(cont.)*

## 4 Develop a **PROCEDURE** to test the hypothesis.

The first thing students must do in developing a procedure (the test plan) is to determine the materials they will need.

They must state exactly what needs to be done in step-by-step order. If they do not place their directions in the right order, or if they leave out a step, it becomes difficult for someone else to follow their directions. A scientist never knows when other scientists will want to try the same experiment to see if they end up with the same results!

*Example: By examining labels on food containers we will see which ones contain seaweed.*

## 5 Record the **RESULTS** of the investigation in written and picture form.

The results (data collected) of a scientific investigation are usually expressed two ways—in written form and in picture form. Both are summary statements. The written form reports the results with words. The picture form (often a chart or graph) reports the results so the information can be understood at a glance.

*Example: The results of the investigation can be recorded on a Data-Capture Sheet provided (page 60).*

## 6 State a **CONCLUSION** that tells what the results of the investigation mean.

The conclusion is a statement which tells the outcome of the investigation. It is drawn after the student has studied the results of the experiment, and it interprets the results in relation to the stated hypothesis. A conclusion statement may read something like either of the following: "The results show that the hypothesis is supported," or "The results show that the hypothesis is not supported." Then restate the hypothesis if it was supported or revise it if it was not supported.

*Example: The hypothesis which stated that we can find seaweed in different food products is either supported (or not supported).*

## 7 Record **QUESTIONS, OBSERVATIONS**, and **SUGGESTIONS** for future investigations.

Students should be encouraged to reflect on the investigations that they complete. These reflections, like those of professional scientists, may produce questions that will lead to further investigations.

*Example: Even though the seaweed was found in some foods, it can be used in others.*

# Science-Process Skills

Even the youngest students blossom in their ability to make sense out of their world and succeed in scientific investigations when they learn and use the science-process skills. These are the tools that help children think and act like professional scientists.

The first five process skills on the list below are the ones that should be emphasized with young children, but all of the skills will be utilized by anyone who is involved in scientific study.

## Observing

It is through the process of observation that all information is acquired. That makes this skill the most fundamental of all the process skills. Children have been making observations all their lives, but they need to be made aware of how they can use their senses and prior knowledge to gain as much information as possible from each experience. Teachers can develop this skill in children by asking questions and making statements that encourage precise observations.

## Communicating

Humans have developed the ability to use language and symbols which allow them to communicate not only in the "here and now" but also over time and space as well. The accumulation of knowledge in science, as in other fields, is due to this process skill. Even young children should be able to understand the importance of researching others' communications about science and the importance of communicating their own findings in ways that are understandable and useful to others. The endangered species journal and the data-capture sheets used in this book are two ways to develop this skill.

## Comparing

Once observation skills are heightened, students should begin to notice the relationships among things that they are observing. *Comparing* means noticing similarities and differences. By asking how things are alike and different or which is smaller or larger, teachers will encourage children to develop their comparison skills.

## Ordering

Other relationships that students should be encouraged to observe are the linear patterns of seriation (order along a continuum: e.g., rough to smooth, large to small, bright to dim, few to many) and sequence (order along a time line or cycle). By ranking graphs, time lines, cyclical and sequence drawings and by putting many objects in order by a variety of properties, students will grow in their abilities to make precise observations about the order of nature.

## Categorizing

When students group or classify objects or events according to logical rationale, they are using the process skill of categorizing. Students begin to use this skill when they group by a single property such as color. As they develop this skill, they will be attending to multiple properties in order to make categorizations; the animal classification system, for example, is one system students can categorize.

# Science-Process Skills *(cont.)*

### Relating
Relating, which is one of the higher-level process skills, requires student scientists to notice how objects and phenomena interact with one another and the changes caused by these interactions. An obvious example of this is the study of chemical reactions.

### Inferring
Not all phenomena are directly observable, because they are out of humankind's reach in terms of time, scale, and space. Some scientific knowledge must be logically inferred based on the data that is available. Much of the work of paleontologists, astronomers, and those studying the structure of matter is done by inference.

### Applying
Even very young, budding scientists should begin to understand that people have used scientific knowledge in practical ways to change and improve the way we live. It is at this application level that science becomes meaningful for many students.

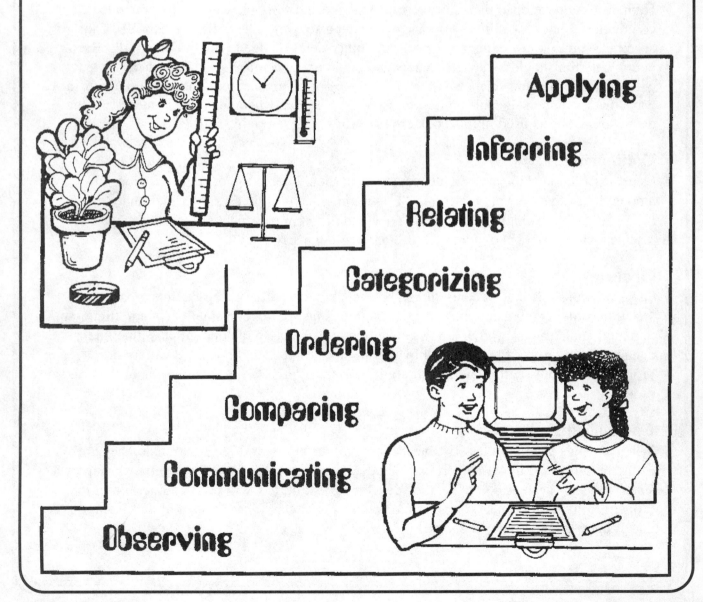

# Organizing Your Unit

## Designing a Science Lesson

In addition to the lessons presented in this unit, you will want to add lessons of your own, lessons that reflect the unique environment in which you live, as well as the interests of your students. When designing new lessons or revising old ones, try to include the following elements in your planning:

### Question

Pose a question to your students that will guide them in the direction of the experiment you wish to perform. Encourage all answers, but you want to lead the students towards the experiment you are going to be doing. Remember, there must be an observation before there can be a question. (Refer to The Scientific Method, pages 5–6.)

### Setting the Stage

Prepare your students for the lesson. Brainstorm to find out what students already know. Have children review books to discover what is already known about the subject. Invite them to share what they have learned.

### Materials Needed for Each Group or Individual

List the materials each group or individual will need for the investigation. Include a data-capture sheet when appropriate.

### Procedure

Make sure students know the steps to take to complete the activity. Whenever possible, ask them to determine the procedure. Make use of assigned roles in group work. Create (or have your students create) a data-capture sheet. Ask yourself, "How will my students record and report what they have discovered? Will they tally, measure, draw, or make a checklist? Will they make a graph? Will they need to preserve specimens?" Let students record results orally, using a videotape or audiotape recorder. For written recording, encourage students to use a variety of paper supplies such as poster board or index cards. It is also important for students to each keep a journal of their investigation activities. Journals can be made of lined and unlined paper. Students can design their own covers. The pages can be stapled or be put together with brads or spiral binding.

### Extensions

Continue the success of the lesson. Consider which related skills or information you can tie into the lesson, like math, language arts skills, or something being learned in social studies. Make curriculum connections frequently and involve the students in making these connections. Extend the activity, whenever possible, to home investigations.

### Closure

Encourage students to think about what they have learned and how the information connects to their own lives. Prepare endangered species journals using directions on page 87. Provide an ample supply of blank and lined pages for students to use as they complete the "Closure" activities. Allow time for students to record their thoughts and pictures in their journals.

# Organizing Your Unit *(cont.)*

## Structuring Student Groups for Scientific Investigations
Using cooperative learning strategies in conjunction with hands-on and discovery learning methods will benefit all the students taking part in the investigation.

## Cooperative Learning Strategies
1. In cooperative learning, all group members need to work together to accomplish the task.
2. Cooperative learning groups should be heterogeneous.
3. Cooperative learning activities need to be designed so that each student contributes to the group and individual group members can be assessed on their performance.
4. Cooperative learning teams need to know the social as well as the academic objectives of a lesson.

## Cooperative Learning Groups
Groups can be determined many ways for the scientific investigations in your class. Here is one way of forming groups that has proven to be successful in primary classrooms.

- **The Team Leader**—scientist in charge of reading directions and setting up equipment.
- **The Biologist**—scientist in charge of carrying out directions (can be more than one student).
- **The Stenographer**—scientist in charge of recording all of the information.
- **The Transcriber**—scientist who translates notes and communicates findings.

If the groups remain the same for more than one investigation, require each group to vary the people chosen for each job. All group members should get a chance to try each job at least once.

## Using Centers for Scientific Investigations
Set up stations for each investigation. To accommodate several groups at a time, stations may be duplicated for the same investigation. Each station should contain directions for the activity, all necessary materials (or a list of materials for investigators to gather), a list of words (a word bank) which students may need for writing and speaking about the experience, and any data-capture sheets or needed materials for recording and reporting data and findings.

Station-to-Station Activities are on pages 78–85. Model and demonstrate each of the activities for the whole group. Have directions at each station. During the modeling session, have a student read the directions aloud while the teacher carries out the activity. When all students understand what they must do, let small groups conduct the investigations at the centers. You may wish to have a few groups working at the centers while others are occupied with other activities. In this case, you will want to set up a rotation schedule so all groups have a chance to work at the centers.

Assign each team to a station, and after they complete the task described, help them rotate in a clockwise order to the other stations. If some groups finish earlier than others, be prepared with another unit-related activity to keep students focused on main concepts. After all rotations have been made by all groups, come together as a class to discuss what was learned.

# Just the Facts

On a sheet of paper list the names of the five oceans. Now examine a globe and you will find the Pacific, Atlantic, Arctic, Antarctic, and Indian Oceans listed. Look more closely, however, and you will discover that the waters are not actually separate. Cartographers have provided arbitrary boundaries for these vast bodies of water. Altogether the oceans cover two-thirds of our planet. That's nearly 145 million square miles—40 times larger than the size of the United States! The Pacific Ocean, which is the biggest and deepest, covers over 64 million square miles and is larger than all of the continents put together. Next largest is the Atlantic whose area is close to 32 million square miles. The Arctic is the smallest of the five and spans only 4.7 million square miles.

Where does all this water come from? Most of its volume arrives from the many rivers of the world. Both the rivers and the ocean are part of a global system known as the water or hydrologic cycle. In this process water evaporates from the ocean and other liquid sources. It condenses into clouds which then drop their rain back onto the land. Rainwater is collected by lakes, streams, and rivers which then flow back into the ocean.

But the ocean is more than just a great expanse of water. First, the ocean is the foundation of life. Scientists believe that life on Earth began in the ocean over 3.5 billion years ago. Water is essential to life and without it we would not be able to survive. It is this great system of water which makes Earth unique among the planets. Ours is the only planet in the solar system which contains vast areas of liquid water.

Second, it is home to a seemingly endless variety of plants and animals that exist only in their watery environment. They range in size from microscopic to some of the largest creatures found on the face of the earth. In the ocean deep are animals that look like plants while others look like stars. Some animals are translucent or neon and seem to glide through the water. Others are yet to be discovered. Many of these species have been around since prehistoric times. People use these plants and animals for food, medicines, and even jewelry.

Third, the ocean is a never-ending series of waves. Every 12 hours the waves rise and fall in tides. These waves contribute to the landscape and weather of the world. They carve cliffs and form beaches. Energy from the waves can even be used to generate electricity. Ocean currents distribute warm and cool air masses around the globe. Sometimes fierce storms or hurricanes are the result.

Finally, the ocean is a thing of beauty to be enjoyed by everyone. It contains a complex system of creatures which exist side-by-side in a most fascinating and unusual world. We must work together to see that the ocean remains that way for future generations.

# What Goes Around Comes Around

## Question

What part does the ocean play in the hydrologic or water cycle?

## Setting the Stage

- Go outside and find a puddle. Mark around its edges with chalk or rocks. Observe the water over the next two days. How long does it take for the water to evaporate? What effect does sunshine or shade have on the process?
- Build a classroom terrarium to observe a miniature water cycle in action.

## Materials Needed for the Class or Each Group

- wet sponge or wet towel
- chalkboard
- heat-resistant dish with lid
- access to a freezer
- hot plate
- data-capture sheet (page 13)

## Procedure *(Student Instructions)*

I. Evaporation—how water gets into the air to form clouds.

1. With the wet sponge or wet towel, draw a large O for ocean on the chalkboard. Watch as it disappears. Where did it go?
2. Repeat the procedure again. This time try to make the O on the chalkboard disappear faster. See what effect fanning it with a towel (to represent the wind) or heating it with a lamp (to imitate the sun's heat) might make.
3. Record your observations on the data-capture sheet.

II. Condensation—how water changes from a vapor to a liquid.

1. About 30 minutes before this exercise put the lid in the freezer.
2. Place the dish on the hot plate and turn the setting on high.
3. When the dish is warm, leave it on the hot plate, but turn off the heat.
4. Take the lid from the freezer and put it on the dish. Observe what happens next.
5. Record your observations on the data-capture sheet.

## Extensions

- Complete the story of the hydrologic cycle. After water has evaporated from the ocean, clouds form. As the droplets become heavier and cool down, they fall to the earth as rain. This water collects in rivers which flow back into the ocean.
- Read *Follow the Water from Brook to Ocean* by Arthur Dorros (Harper Collins, 1991).

## Closure

In their ocean journals, have the students write a story about the journey of a water drop as it goes through the water cycle.

# What Goes Around Comes Around (cont.)

## I. Evaporation

1. Explain what happened to the water in the O you drew on the board.

_____

2. Tell how you tried to make the second O disappear faster._____

_____

_____

3. How do you think water from the ocean is evaporated? _____

_____

4. Conclusion. Two ways to speed up evaporation are _____

_____

## II. Condensation

1. Predict what will happen when the cold lid is placed on the warm dish.

_____

_____

2. Recall what happened when the cold lid was placed on the warm dish.

_____

Where did the water come from? _____

_____

3. What happened to the water droplets?_____

_____

4. Conclusion. Water droplets fall back down into the pan when_____

_____

On the back of this paper draw a picture of the hydrologic cycle. First, draw a mountain near the ocean and a river flowing down the mountain.  Then draw a sun in the sky to show how the ocean water is heated.  As water from the ocean evaporates, water droplets form clouds. Draw some clouds in the sky.  As the droplets become heavier and are cooled by the wind, they drop moisture on the earth. Draw some rain from the clouds. Rainwater collects in the rivers, which flow back into the ocean.  Color the river blue.

# A Salty Solution

## Question

How do we know that there is salt in the ocean?

## Setting the Stage

- Bring in a box of salt. Pour a sample for each student. Have them examine the crystals by tasting, feeling, and smelling them. Make a class chart to describe the salt.
- Discuss what salt is and how it is used in daily life.

## Materials Needed for Each Individual or Small Group

- aluminum pie plate
- 1 cup (250 mL) ocean water (If none is available, prepare your own ahead of time by mixing 1 tsp. (5 mL) of salt to each cup of water.)
- data-capture sheet (page 15)

## Procedure *(Student Instructions)*

1. Pour the cup of salt water into the aluminum pie plate.
2. Place your plate in a warm, dry place.
3. Allow several days for the water to dry up.
4. Examine what you find after all the water has evaporated. How does the residue feel? What does it look like? How does it smell and taste?
5. Complete the data-capture sheet. With a three-hole punch, make holes along the left side of your sheet.
6. Add your page to the class three-ring binder.

## Extensions

- With a magnifying glass, examine salt crystals. Draw pictures of salt crystals.
- Examine some other crystals—sugar, rock candy, quartz, for example. Compare them with salt crystals.
- Grow your own crystals. Dissolve two cups (500 mL) of granulated sugar in 3/4 cup (188 mL) of boiling water. Let the solution cool before pouring it into clear plastic cups. Observe daily. Crystals can also be produced by mixing enough baking soda with hot water until no more dissolves. Pour into a clear jar.

## Closure

In their ocean journals, have students write a description of salt without using the name. For example, the tiny, white grains of this coarse substance are important in preserving and seasoning foods. It is found in ocean water. Despite its strong taste, it is a necessary nutrient for our bodies.

# A Salty Solution *(cont.)*

**Directions:** After examining your salt crystals write descriptions in each section of the chart below.

## Characteristics of Salt

| | |
|---|---|
| **Appearance** | |
| **Smell** | |
| **Taste** | |
| **Feel** | |
| **Other** | |

# Afloat

## Question

Why is it easier to swim in salt water than in fresh water?

## Setting the Stage

- What rivers, ponds, lakes, or other bodies of water are close by? Are they fresh water or salt water? What is the difference between the two types of water?
- Discuss with students any experiences they have had swimming in the ocean. Compare it with experiences swimming in a pool, lake, or pond. In which type of water was it easier to swim?

## Materials Needed for Each Individual or Group

- two identical glasses or clear plastic cups
- tap water
- salt water (Prepare some ahead of time by adding one tsp. [5 mL] of salt to each cup of water.)
- one fresh egg or small potato
- data-capture sheet (page 17)

## Procedure *(Student Instructions)*

1. Fill one glass with tap water.
2. Pour an equal amount of salt water into the second glass.
3. Predict what will happen when the egg is placed into each glass. Record the predictions on the data-capture sheet.
4. Place the egg into the glass of tap water. What happens? Record the results on the data-capture sheet.
5. Remove the egg from the fresh water and place it in the glass of salt water. What happens? Record the results on the data-capture sheet. (If the egg doesn't float, add more salt to the water.)
6. Write your conclusions about the experiment on the data-capture sheet.

## Extensions

- During the above experiment, ask students what they think might happen if the salt water contained even more salt. Add one teaspoon (5 mL) of salt to the glass at a time. Observe how it affects the position of the egg. Ask students how the amount of salt in water affects a person's ability to swim.
- Have the students find out why it is so easy to float in the Dead Sea.

## Closure

In their ocean journals, have the students write a story about the fish that couldn't float until it found the right type of water.

# Afloat *(cont.)*

**Predictions**

a. What will happen when the egg is placed in the glass filled with tap water?

_____

_____

b. What will happen when the egg is placed in the glass filled with salt water?

_____

_____

**Results**

a. This is what happened when the egg was placed in the glass filled with tap water: _____

_____

b. This is what happened when the egg was placed in the glass filled with salt water:_____

_____

**Conclusions**

This experiment led to the conclusion that _____

_____

Draw a picture of the egg in the glass of tap water on the left. Draw the egg in the glass of salt water on the right. Label each glass.

Tap Water                                    Salt Water

# Frozen Seawater

## Question

Why doesn't the ocean in areas other than the Arctic and Antarctic freeze over solid?

## Setting the Stage

- On a map or globe, identify the oceans. Where can frozen ocean water be found? Ask the students if the rest of the ocean ever freezes over. Record their responses and save; refer to it after the experiment to see how many were correct.
- Discuss why salt is sometimes scattered on icy roads.

## Materials Needed for the Class or Each Group

- several small plastic bags (ones you can tie shut)
- several rubber bands
- a freezer thermometer
- tap water
- table salt or sea salt
- one cup measuring cup
- teaspoon
- access to a freezer
- data-capture sheet (page 19)

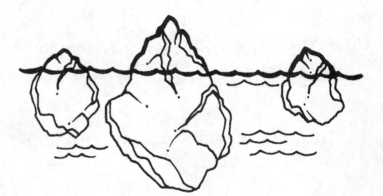

## Procedure *(Student Instructions)*

1. Pour one cup (250 mL) of tap water into a plastic bag.
2. Place the bulb end of the thermometer into the center of the bag and fasten securely with a rubber band.
3. Put the bag in the freezer. Check on it after 15 minutes.
4. Continue to check on the water every 15 minutes until the water in the bag begins to form ice.
5. Read the temperature on the thermometer, and record it on your data-capture sheet.
6. Mix one teaspoon (5 mL) of salt or sea salt with one cup of water and pour the mixture into a plastic bag.
7. Place the thermometer in the bag as directed above and check on the the water every 15 minutes.
8. On your data-capture sheet, record the temperature as soon as the salt water begins to freeze.
9. Compare the freezing points of tap water and salt water.

## Extension

Find out if salinity (the percentage of salt dissolved in ocean water) affects the freezing point of water. Add two or more teaspoons (10 mL) of salt to one cup (250 mL) of water before pouring it into a plastic bag. Follow the same procedure as outlined above.

## Closure

In their ocean journals, have the students draw and label two thermometers—one to show the freezing point of tap water and the other to show the freezing point of salt water.

# Frozen Seawater *(cont.)*

### Observations—Tap Water

1. What changes were there after the first 15 minutes?

   _____

   _____

2. How long did it take for the water in the bag to begin to freeze?

   _____

### Observations—Salt Water

1. What changes were there after the first 15 minutes?

   _____

   _____

2. How long did it take for the water in the bag to begin to freeze?

   _____

Color in the temperature at which the water began to freeze.

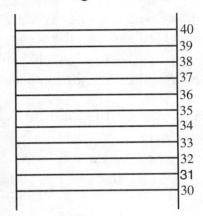

Color in the temperature at which the water began to freeze.

### Comparisons

1. Which water froze at the lower temperature? _____

2. Explain the effects that salt has on the freezing point of water.

   _____

   _____

   _____

# The Ocean Blue

## Question

Why is the ocean blue?

## Setting the Stage

- Look at a map or globe. Ask the students how much of the Earth is covered by water. What color is used to depict the ocean? What different colors are used to depict other bodies of water?
- When astronauts in space observe the Earth, they see a shining blue-white disk. What are the blue forms that the astronauts see? What accounts for the white forms that they see?
- Make a prism. Place a glass of water in sunlight. Move the glass until a rainbow of colors appears on the wall or ceiling. Review the colors of the spectrum.

## Materials Needed for Each Group

- glass or plastic bottle
- water
- a few drops of milk
- a flashlight
- data-capture sheet (page 21)

## Procedure (Student Instructions)

1. As you complete each step, record your observations on the data-capture sheet.
2. Fill the bottle about 3/4 full with tap water. Observe the color of the water as it is poured into the bottle.
3. Add a few drops of milk to the water. What happens to the water? (Note: The milk represents suspended particles in the ocean.)
4. Shine the flashlight against the side of the bottle. What color does the mixture appear? (Note: The flashlight represents the sun.)

## Extensions

- Make sure the students understand that the color of an object is determined by the degree in which it absorbs or scatters light. When sunlight hits the ocean, blue light is absorbed and the other colors scatter. To our eyes the water appears blue.
- In some places around the world, the ocean is green. Have the students find out what causes some ocean water to be green. Learn about some other causes that affect the color of ocean water (for example, living organisms, muddy rivers that flow into the ocean, plankton, algae, or debris).

## Closure

In their ocean journals, students can write a paragraph about some things that affect the color of the ocean.

# The Ocean Blue (cont.)

1. What color is the water you poured into the bottle?

   _____

2. What happens when the drops of milk are added to the water?

   _____

   _____

3. What color is the light from the flashlight?

   _____

4. What happened when the flashlight was shined against the side of the bottle?

   _____

   _____

   _____

5. On the diagram below, write the names of the colors that appear on the other side of the prism.

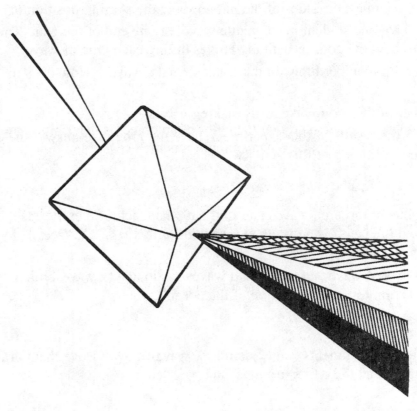

# Surf's Up!

**Question**

How do waves move?

**Setting the Stage**

- Ask students what they know about waves. Record their responses on chart paper or the chalkboard.
- Demonstrate wave action with this activity. Give each pair of students a length of rope. Tell one partner in each pair to hold the rope still while the other partner moves the rope in an up-and-down manner. Tie a ribbon to any point on the rope and manipulate the rope again. Discuss their observations.

**Materials Needed for the Class or Each Group**

- pencil
- pan of water (the pan should be at least 2 feet [60 cm] long)
- a cork or floating bath toy
- masking tape
- data-capture sheet (page 23)

**Procedure** *(Student Instructions)*

1. On the data-capture sheet write True or False after each statement. Decide your answers as a whole group.
2. When the sheet has been completed, place the cork or bath toy in the pan of water.
3. With masking tape, mark the sides of the pan to show the starting position of the cork or bath toy.
4. In each group, have one student make gentle waves at one end of the pan. Then make rough waves. Observe how the cork or bath toy moves during each type of wave.
5. Have another group member blow on the water to make waves. How does the cork or bath toy move now?
6. Let each member of the group take turns making waves.
7. After discussing the results of this experiment, have the groups re-answer the questionnaire they completed at the beginning of this activity.

**Extensions**

- Direct the students to research waves and find out what each of these terms means: wavelength, trough, crest, and breakers. An excellent resource for this lesson is *Oceans* by Seymour Simon (Morrow Junior Books, 1990).
- Discuss other types of wave action—sound waves, radio and tv waves, microwaves, etc. Compare their action to the wave action of the ocean's waters.

**Closure**

In their ocean journals, students can explain how waves move. Have them draw a picture of three or four waves and label the crests, troughs, and wavelengths.

22

# Surf's Up! *(cont.)*

Before you begin your experiment, read each statement about wave action. As a group determine if the statement is True or False. Write True or False in the space provided under the Before column. After the experiment has been completed, read each statement again. Write True or False in the After column.

| | Before | After |
|---|---|---|
| 1. Waves move in an up-and-down motion. | | |
| 2. An object sitting on top of a wave will be moved forward. | | |
| 3. Winds cannot make waves. | | |
| 4. Waves follow one another, forming a train of waves. | | |
| 5. Waves move water from one part of the ocean to another. | | |
| 6. Waves travel through water. | | |
| 7. The stronger the wind, the bigger the wave. | | |
| 8. Rough waves and gentle waves will move an object differently through the water. | | |
| 9. A wave has a high point. | | |
| 10. Waves move from side to side. | | |

# Current Events

## Question

How does an ocean current move?

## Setting the Stage

Share the following information with students: It was Benjamin Franklin who helped ships sail the Atlantic Ocean more quickly. How? Franklin observed that vessels crossing the Atlantic at the far north were slower than those following another route. He learned that a powerful current flowed toward Europe along this northern route. A ship sailing against this current would have a longer journey than one sailing with it. Franklin mapped the current which we now know as the Gulf Stream.

## Materials Needed for the Class or Each Group

- two, 1-pint (.5L) milk bottles or carafes
- 6 or more 5" x 7" (12.5 cm x 17.5 cm) index cards
- salt
- 1/2 teaspoon (2.5 mL) measuring spoon
- red food coloring
- spoon for mixing
- access to a sink or a large plastic container
- data-capture sheet (page 25)

## Procedure *(Student Instructions)*

1. Fill both bottles to the top with water.
2. Add 1/2 teaspoon (2.5 mL) of salt and one drop of food coloring to one bottle of water; mix it thoroughly with the spoon.
3. Put the plain bottle of water in the sink or pan.
4. Stand over the sink or pan as you do this next step. Place an index card on top of the bottle of colored water and quickly turn it over. Air pressure should be holding the card in place. If not, try again.
5. Place this bottle on top of the bottle of water in the sink. Remove the index card and observe what happens.
6. Repeat the experiment. This time place the bottle of colored salt water in the sink and the other bottle on top of it. Remove the card and observe.
7. Record your observations on the data-capture sheet.

## Extensions

- Study how currents are important: they help transport boats, they affect the climate of nearby lands, and they transport fish that are too young to swim great distances.
- For more information about Benjamin Franklin and the Gulf Stream, read *The Atlantic Ocean* by Susan Heinrichs (Childrens Press, 1986).

## Closure

In their ocean journals, students can draw a map of the oceans closest to their continent and label the ocean currents of those waters.

# Current Events *(cont.)*

**Directions:** Next to each picture describe what happened to the water in the bottles.  Color the water to show the action that took place.

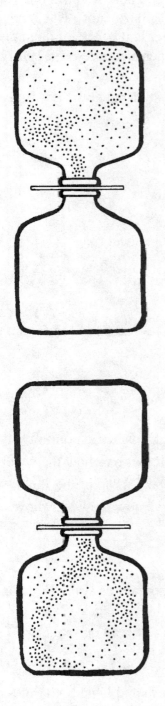

_____

_____

_____

_____

_____

_____

_____

_____

_____

_____

_____

_____

_____

# Hot and Cold Currents

## Question

How does water temperature affect ocean currents?

## Setting the Stage

- Set up this demonstration to show the differences between hot and cold water. Pour 1/4 (60 mL) cup of cold water and 1/4 cup (60 mL) of hot water into identical-size cups. Have the students predict which one will freeze faster. Place both cups in a freezer and check on them every five minutes. Which one freezes first? Explain that in this next experiment they will learn how water temperature affects ocean currents.

- Review how salt content (salinity) affects ocean currents. Ask students how they think water temperature would affect ocean currents.

## Materials Needed for Each Group

- red food coloring
- water
- mixing bowl
- spoon for mixing
- ice cube tray
- freezer
- baking pan
- pepper
- data-capture sheet (page 27)

## Procedure *(Student Instructions)*

1. Prepare the ice cubes ahead of time. In the mixing bowl add a few drops of red food coloring to the water.
2. Mix with the spoon and pour into the ice cube tray.
3. Place the tray into the freezer.
4. Fill the baking pan with warm (not hot) water.
5. Sprinkle the surface of the water with pepper to help you track the water's motion.
6. Put one red ice cube into the water at one end of the baking pan; observe how the water moves.
7. Empty the pan. Fill it with warm water and sprinkle some pepper on top of the water.
8. This time place one red ice cube at each end of the pan. Observe how the water moves.
9. Record your observations on the data-capture sheet.

## Extensions

- Compare the temperature of water at both Poles with water temperatures at the Equator. Have the students explain the differences.
- Find out what role the Earth's rotation has in shaping the paths of ocean currents.

## Closure

In their ocean journals, have the students draw a diagram of Earth and label both Poles and the Equator. Write a paragraph describing how ocean waters move among them.

# Hot and Cold Currents *(cont.)*

## Experiment I

Draw and color a picture to show how you think the water in the pan will move when a red ice cube is added to the water.

In which direction did the cold water move? _____

_____

What happened to the cold water as it warmed up? _____

_____

How did the surface water move as the cold water moved along the bottom?

_____

## Experiment 2

Draw and color a picture to show how you think the water in the pan will move when two red ice cubes are added to the water.

In which direction did the cold water move? _____

_____

What happened to the cold water as it warmed up? _____

_____

How did the surface water move as the cold water moved along the bottom?

_____

# Heavier and Heavier

## Question

Is water pressure greater at the ocean bottom?

## Setting the Stage

- Review with the students the concept of gravity. Throw an orange into the air and catch it. Ask students why it came down. Discuss other examples of gravity in action.

- Also review air pressure with this demonstration. Spread a sheet of newspaper flat on a table. Slide a ruler under one edge. Ask students to predict what will happen when you hit the end of the ruler that is not under the newspaper. Hit the ruler with your fist. The weight of the air pressing down on the paper makes it difficult for the paper to be lifted up.

## Materials Needed for the Class or Each Group

- 2 clean, empty, plastic soft drink bottles
- nail, knitting needle, or other utensil to make holes in the bottles
- masking tape
- 2 blocks of wood
- sink with running water
- salt water (To make some, add 1 tsp. [5 mL] of salt to each cup of water.)
- data-capture sheet (page 29)

## Procedure *(Student Instructions)*

1. With the nail make three holes in the bottle—one near the top, one in the middle, and one near the bottom.
2. Tape the holes. Fill one bottle with tap water and the other with salt water.
3. Stand each bottle on a block of wood in the sink.
4. Predict how the water will spurt from each hole in the bottle filled with tap water. Predict differences in the salt water-filled bottle.
5. Remove the tape and observe and compare the distance that the water spurts from each hole in the two bottles.
6. Complete the data-capture sheet.

## Extension

Give students the following information: Some deep-sea animals live seven miles (11 km) below the ocean's surface. Water pressure here is more than eight tons per square inch. What do the students suppose will happen if these animals were to be brought up suddenly to the ocean surface? What happens when deep-sea divers are brought up too suddenly to the water's surface? What is the treatment for someone with the "bends"?

## Closure

In their ocean journals, have the students construct a chart to show how differently the tap water and salt water moved through the holes in the bottles.

28

# Heavier and Heavier *(cont.)*

**Directions:** Predict how the water will flow from each hole.

1. In which bottle will water from the top hole flow farther?

2. In which bottle will water from the middle hole flow farther?

3. In which bottle will water from the bottom hole flow farther?

| Tap Water | Salt Water |
|---|---|
|  |  |
|  |  |
|  |  |

Record the results of the experiment.

1. Water from the top hole flowed farther in this bottle.

2. Water from the middle hole flowed farther in this bottle.

3. Water from the bottom hole flowed farther in this bottle.

| Tap Water | Salt Water |
|---|---|
|  |  |
|  |  |
|  |  |

Draw the water as it spurted out of each hole in the two bottles.

tap water 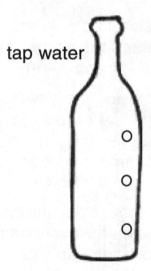 salt water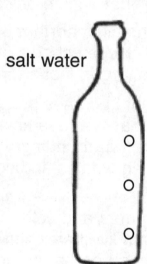

On the lines below, compare the action of the salt water with the tap water in the two bottles.

_____

_____

_____

_____

# Just the Facts

In ancient times sailors were afraid to move out of sight of land. They thought that the ocean was full of monsters and other unknown dangers. Some of their fears were justified. After all, people then did not have the sophisticated nautical instruments that are now available. Nor did they have the knowledge about land forms, icebergs, ocean currents, and waves that may have helped them have safer journeys.

Today diving equipment, scuba gear, satellites, and submersibles help us learn about what is in the ocean and on the ocean floor. In 1960 the Trieste, a bathyscaphe, carried two men nearly seven miles below the surface of the Pacific. It is, so far, the deepest place found in the ocean but man is still exploring. Now satellites orbiting hundreds of miles above Earth gather various kinds of information about the ocean including surface water temperature, location of schools of fish, wind speed, water depth, and the movement of oil spills.

Modern technology has helped scientists form a better picture of what actually lies in the ocean. Here is a brief outline of life beneath the waves.

- The Sunlit Zone contains all-important plankton, microscopic plants that start off the food chain. Huge schools of fish such as sardines and herring, share these waters with larger, fast-swimming fish like tuna and swordfish.

- In the Midwaters the light becomes progressively darker, and the water becomes colder. Fish that live here have developed efficient senses to help them survive in their surroundings. Some fish even carry lights on their bodies! Deep-diving whales and schools of squid make this level their home.

- At the Bottom it is pitch dark and cold. Soft mud or sediment covers the ocean floor. Animals that live here feed on other creatures that flow past them from the upper ocean or that are found in the sediment. Sponges, brittle stars, and sea anemones are typical animals found here.

Besides the ecosystems in the ocean there are numerous land forms on the ocean floor. The Continental Shelf surrounds our land and gently slopes downward from the shore to form the Continental Slope to the ocean floor. Some deep, dark trenches can be found on the floor as well as mountain ranges and some volcanoes. When these mountains break the ocean's surface, they form islands. It is interesting to note that the deepest valleys and the tallest mountains on Earth can be found under the ocean.

There are many mysteries in the ocean, and scientists are still trying to figure them out. With new technology and equipment being developed all the time, they may be able to conquer this vast and mysterious underwater world.

# The Sandy Shore

## Question

What materials can be found in sand on the shore? How is sand formed?

## Setting the Stage

- Bring in some sand. Give a cupful to each group and allow them to explore its characteristics. As a whole group make a chart of the information that was gathered.

- Give each student a piece of hard candy. Before they are allowed to eat it, discuss what will happen when they leave the candy in their mouths and suck on it. What causes the candy to become smoother? Let them pop the candy into their mouths; caution them not to chew. Examine the pieces every five minutes until they are dissolved; discuss the changes taking place.

## Materials Needed for Each Group

- small rocks
- small seashells
- glass jar with lid
- water
- data-capture sheet (page 32)

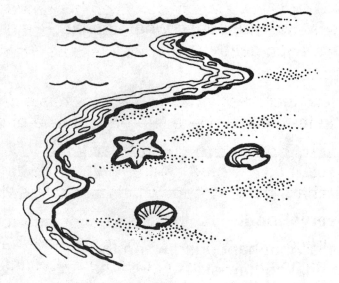

## Procedure *(Student Instructions)*

1. Place some rocks and seashells into the glass jar.
2. Add enough water to fill the jar about 2/3 full.
3. Tightly fasten the lid.
4. Gently shake the jar. What happens?
5. Shake the jar more vigorously. What happens now?
6. Complete the data-capture sheet.

## Extensions

- Give each group of students a handful of small seashells, a hammer, and a sheet of newspaper. Direct them to place the seashells in the center of the newspaper and fold the paper over the shells. Strike the shells with the hammer a number of times. Unfold the newspaper to see the beginnings of sand. Have the students explain how the ocean waves help make sand.

- Place a few stones in a water-filled glass jar. Ask the students to predict how long it will take before the stones form sand. Place the jar on a shelf and make records of your daily observations. At the end of a week discuss with students what happened. Establish that it is the ocean waves which pound repeatedly against the rocks and shells on shore which produce sand.

## Closure

In their ocean journals, have students glue some sand to the top of a page. Tell them to write the story of how it was created.

# The Sandy Shore *(cont.)*

## Observation I

This is what happened when water was added to the rocks and shells in the jar.

_____

_____

This is how the rocks and shells looked in the jar.

## Observation II

This is what happened when the jar was shaken gently.

_____

_____

_____

This is how the rocks and shells looked when the jar was shaken gently.

## Observation III

This is what happened when the jar was shaken harder.

_____

_____

This is how the rocks and shells looked when the jar was shaken harder.

## Conclusion

This is how sand is formed in the ocean: _____

_____

_____

# Our Changing Shore Line

## Question

How does the ocean change the shape of our shore line?

## Setting the Stage

Set up a demonstration for the whole class. Note: You may want to go outdoors for this activity. On a piece of heavy cardboard or particle board, make a mountain of dirt. All at once pour some water on top of the dirt; observe. Now spray some water at the bottom of the dirt mountain (use a squirt gun or spray bottle); observe. Discuss the observations. Explain that the ocean changes the shape of our coastline in a similar manner.

## Materials Needed for Each Group

- large bowl for mixing
- dirt, sand, or both
- water
- dish pan
- data-capture sheet (page 34)

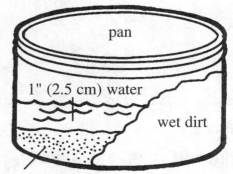

pan

1" (2.5 cm) water

wet dirt

1" (2.5 cm) dirt or sand

## Procedure *(Student Instructions)*

1. In the bowl mix the dirt or sand with enough water to make a thick mud.
2. Make a sloping pile of the wet dirt on one-half of the inside of the pan as shown in the diagram.
3. Pat it down into a solid mass.
4. Allow the structure to dry for two or more days.
5. When the structure is dry, pour a 1" (2.5 cm) layer of dirt or sand on the bottom of the pan that is not already covered (see diagram).
6. Pour about 1" (2.5 cm) of water on top of this layer of dirt or sand.
7. With your hand or an object, make waves in the water. Observe.
8. Make some larger waves. Observe.
9. Record your observations on the data-capture sheet.

## Extensions

- Have the students research what effect incoming tides might have on the movement of sand on the beach.
- Read more details about how beaches are formed in the book *The Oceans* by David Lambert (The Bookwright Press, 1984).

## Closure

In their ocean journals, have the students write an explanation of how waves help shape the beach.

# Our Changing Shore Line (cont.)

**Directions:** Draw a diagram of your experiment. Label the parts that represent the shore, the ocean, and the ocean floor.

## Observation 1

What happened when the waves hit the shore line? _____

_____

_____

## Observation 2

What happened to the shore line when larger waves were made?

_____

_____

## Explanation

How does this experiment explain what happens to the shore line at the beach?

_____

_____

_____

# Underwater Plants

**Question**

What do underwater plants need in order to grow?

**Setting the Stage**

- Show the students a number of pictures of underwater plants. How many can they identify?
- With the students, review what land plants need in order to survive. List those factors on the chalkboard. Which of these are necessary for underwater plants to survive?
- Discuss the differences between land plants and underwater plants.

**Materials Needed for Each Group or the Class**

- masking tape
- black marking pen
- 3 of the same rooted underwater plants (available from a tropical fish store)
- #2 or #3 gravel (available from a tropical fish store)
- 3 small fish bowls or tall glass jars
- water
- black construction paper
- aluminum foil or plastic wrap
- plant food
- measuring stick
- data-capture sheet (page 36)

**Procedure** *(Student Instructions)*

1. With the marking pen and masking tape, make labels for the three bowls: #1, #2, and #3. Attach one to each bowl.
2. Layer the bottom of each container with 2–3 inches (5–8 cm) of gravel.
3. Plant one underwater plant in each container and fill with water. Keep the water temperature between 70–75 degrees F (21–24 degrees C).
4. Place container #1 near a good source of light, and add plant food to it every other day.
5. Surround the sides and top of container #2 with black construction paper so that no light can get in.
6. Wrap aluminum foil around the top of container #3 so that no air can get in.
7. Observe the plants for a period of one week. Record beginning and ending observations on the data-capture sheet.

**Extensions**

- What effect does pollution have on underwater plants? Add a different contaminant such as paint or oil to the water of each plant, and observe the effects over a period of time.
- Learn more about seaweed, which are among the tallest plants in the world. How and where do they grow? How are they beneficial to man? An excellent resource is *Monster Seaweeds: The Story of the Giant Kelps* by Mary Daegling (Macmillan, 1987).

**Closure**

Have the students draw a picture of an underwater plant in their ocean journals. Tell them to write a paragraph explaining what these plants need in order to grow.

# Underwater Plants *(cont.)*

**Directions:** Compare the **Before** and **After** of each plant.  Write descriptions in the spaces provided.

| **Before** | **After** |
|---|---|
| Plant #1<br><br>Height _____<br><br>Appearance _____<br><br>_____<br><br>_____<br><br>_____ | Plant #1<br><br>Height _____<br><br>Appearance _____<br><br>_____<br><br>Why it did/did not survive: _____<br><br>_____ |
| **Before** | **After** |
| Plant #2<br><br>Height _____<br><br>Appearance _____<br><br>_____<br><br>_____<br><br>_____ | Plant #2<br><br>Height _____<br><br>Appearance _____<br><br>_____<br><br>Why it did/did not survive: _____<br><br>_____ |
| **Before** | **After** |
| Plant #3<br><br>Height _____<br><br>Appearance _____<br><br>_____<br><br>_____ | Plant #3<br><br>Height _____<br><br>Appearance _____<br><br>_____<br><br>Why it did/did not survive: _____<br><br>_____ |

# Mollusks Vs. Crustaceans

**Question?**

What is the difference between a mollusk and a crustacean?

**Setting the Stage**

Ask the students if they have ever eaten lobster, crab, mussels, or clams. Describe how these animals look and feel on the outside. Write the students' descriptive words and phrases on chart paper and save for later reference.

**Materials Needed for Each Group**

- one lobster, crab, or shrimp (skeleton left on)
- one clam, scallop, or mussel (already opened)
- data-capture sheet (page 38)

**Procedure** *(Student Instructions)*

1. Closely observe both animals before recording answers on the data-capture sheet.
2. At the top of the data-capture sheet, write the name of each animal you will be comparing.
3. Read the first description on the data-capture sheet.
4. As a group decide which of the two animals best fits that description.
5. Write the animal's name in the space.
6. Go on to the second statement and decide on an answer.
7. Continue until all the statements have been read.
8. Write a group conclusion on the lines provided.

**Extensions**

- Compare the mollusk and the crustacean used in the experiment. Draw a Venn diagram to show their likenesses and differences.
- Explain that some mollusks are bivalves. Write some of these words on the chalkboard for all to see: biplane, biannual, binary, biweekly, bilingual, bicycle, binoculars. Have the students identify the common prefix in all the words. What does it mean? What does each word mean? What do they think bivalve means?
- As a class, cook some clam chowder.
- What are echinoderms? What are arthropods? Examine some other types of ocean animals.

**Closure**

In their ocean journals, have the students draw a picture of their favorite crustacean or bivalve along with a paragraph explaining what is a bivalve or a crustacean.

# Mollusks Vs. Crustaceans (cont.)

**Directions**: On the lines below write the names of the two animals you are going to compare.

#1 _____     #2 _____

Now read each pair of statements below. Write the name of the animal that best fits that description on the line. Make your decision as a whole group. When you have read all the statements, write a conclusion about each animal.

| Column A | Column B |
|---|---|
| 1. They have a hard, outside shell.<br><br>_____ | 1. An exoskeleton covers its body.<br><br>_____ |
| 2. Soft-bodied animals live inside a shell.<br><br>_____ | 2. They have soft bodies.<br><br>_____ |
| 3. Some are bivalves and have a two-piece shell.<br><br>_____ | 3. They have a number of body segments.<br><br>_____ |
| 4. They have a smooth interior.<br><br>_____ | 4. They have at least five pairs of legs.<br><br>_____ |

## CONCLUSIONS

Column A lists characteristics of mollusks. Column B lists characteristics of crustaceans.

Which animal is the mollusk? _____

How did you come to this conclusion? _____

_____

Which animal is the crustacean? _____

How did you come to this conclusion? _____

_____

# Leagues Under the Sea

## Question

How can submarines go deep below the ocean's surface and come back up again?

## Setting the Stage

- Write the word "bathysphere" on the chalkboard. Ask the students to define the word. Establish that a bathysphere is a spherical diving machine developed in 1930 by William Beebe. With it divers could reach a deeper level than they had previously been able. Today, research vehicles known as submersibles are used to carry people and equipment to the deepest ocean levels.
- Discuss how scuba gear helps people explore the ocean depths. What do the letters in the word scuba stand for?

## Materials Needed for Each Individual

- eyedropper
- clear-plastic soda bottle with a cap
- water
- a tall glass (plastic is fine)
- data-capture sheet (page 40)

## Procedure *(Student Instructions)*

1. Fill the plastic bottle almost to the top with water and then set it aside.
2. Pour water into the glass and add the eyedropper.
3. Fill the dropper with enough water (by squeezing its bulb) so that the top of the bulb just floats at the surface of the water.
4. Carefully lift the dropper along its tube and place it in the plastic bottle of water.
5. Securely attach the bottle top.
6. Predict what will happen when the outside of the bottle is squeezed. Write your predictions on the data-capture sheet.
7. Squeeze the outside of the bottle. Observe the movement of the dropper. Draw your observations on the data-capture sheet.

## Extensions

- Learn about the famous oceanographer Jacques Cousteau. Read the book *Jacques Cousteau: Man of the Oceans* by Carole Greene (Childrens Press, 1990) or find articles in *National Geographic* magazine (have your librarian help you).
- Jacques Cousteau was co-inventor of the aqualung. Find out more about this invention in the book *Free Flight Undersea* by Paul Westman (Dillon Press, 1980).
- For more information about submersibles, see *Oceanography* by Martyn Bramwell (Hampstead Press, 1989) or *From Space to the Seabed* by Jonathan Rawlinson (Rourke Enterprises, Inc., 1988).

## Closure

In their ocean journals, students can write a description of how submarines are able to descend and then come back up from the ocean bottom.

# Leagues Under the Sea *(cont.)*

**Before**

Predict what will happen when the outside of the bottle is squeezed.

_____

_____

In which direction will the dropper move? _____

_____

What will happen to the water level inside the dropper when the bottle
is squeezed? _____

_____

What will happen to the dropper when the outside of the bottle is released?

_____

_____

**After**

In the space below, draw a picture of the dropper in the bottle.  With red arrows
show how the dropper moved when the bottle was squeezed.  Draw green
arrows to show how the dropper moved when the bottle was released.

40

# Mineral Deposits

## Question

How are mineral deposits formed on the ocean floor?

## Setting the Stage

- Write the following words on the chalkboard or overhead projector: manganese, sand, copper, nickel, cobalt, oil, sulfur, and gravel. Ask the students to explain how these resources are related to the ocean.
- With the class, brainstorm a list of some other resources we get from the ocean besides those listed above.

## Materials Needed for Each Individual

- small stones or pebbles
- aluminum pie pan (or other deep container)
- 2 cups (500 mL)of warm water
- 1/2 cup (125 mL) of granulated sugar
- bowl and spoon
- data-capture sheet (page 42)

## Procedure *(Student Instructions)*

1. Arrange the rocks close together in the center of the pie pan.
2. In the bowl mix the water and sugar thoroughly.
3. Pour the water mixture over the stones.
4. Observe what happens over a number of days.
5. Record your observations on the data-capture sheet.

## Extensions

- Look for other examples in nature in which layer is built upon layer (sedimentary rocks or a tree stump, for example).
- Discuss the various methods used to gather resources, such as kelp and oil from the ocean.
- Discuss the uses of the various resources gathered from the ocean. For example, kelp or seaweed can be used as a food and also as fertilizer.
- For more information about the ocean's resources read *The Continental Shelf* by Alice Gilbreath (Dillon Press, Inc., 1986).

## Closure

In their ocean journals, have the students draw a picture of an actual manganese nodule found on the ocean bottom.

# Mineral Deposits *(cont.)*

**Directions:** In each section draw a picture of the changes you observed.

| **Day 1** | **Day _____** |
|---|---|
| | |
| **Day _____** | **Day _____** |
| | |
| **Day _____** | **Day _____** |
| | |

# Floating Ice

**Question**

What is an iceberg?

**Setting the Stage**

- Share the following paragraph with the students: A glacier is a huge sheet of ice that never melts. Some states like Montana and Alaska have glaciers. The largest glaciers, however, can be found in the Polar regions of the world. When a chunk of glacier falls into the ocean it becomes an iceberg.

- Ask students to identify the ocean liner, *Titanic*. Establish that in 1912 the ship was on its first voyage from London to New York. In the Atlantic Ocean, it hit an iceberg and the ship sank. Of the 2,200 aboard, 1,500 drowned. (Interested students may want to read *Exploring the Titanic* by Robert D. Ballard, Scholastic, 1988.)

**Materials Needed for Each Individual**

- plastic bag and its tie
- freezer
- scissors
- deep pan of water (Only one will be needed for each group of students.)
- measuring tape or ruler
- data-capture sheet (page 44)

**Procedure** *(Student Instructions)*

1. Carefully fill the plastic bag about 2/3 full with water and then tie the end.
2. Place the plastic bag in the freezer overnight.
3. Remove the frozen mass from the bag.
4. Predict what will happen when the ice is placed in the pan of water.
5. Place the ice in the water. Observe what happens. How does it compare to your predictions? How much of the ice mass is floating above water?
6. Record your observations on the data-capture sheet.

**Extension**

Make a file of "Iceberg Facts." Give each student a large sheet of drawing paper. Instruct them to fold the paper into fourths. Direct them to find out and write an interesting fact about icebergs in each section on their paper. Illustrate the facts and compile them in a special class scrapbook or file folder. Continue to add to it as new facts are learned. Two excellent resources for this activity are *Icebergs and Glaciers* by Seymour Simon (William Morrow and Company, Inc., 1987) and *Danger—Icebergs!* by Roma Gans (Thomas Y. Crowell, 1987).

**Closure**

In their ocean journals, have the students describe an iceberg. Tell how an iceberg can be dangerous to ocean travelers.

# Floating Ice *(cont.)*

**Before**

Predict what will happen when you place your iceberg in the pan of water.

_____

Predict how much of your iceberg will float above water when it is placed in the pan. Write your estimated measurement on the line.

_____

**After**

Measure how much of the iceberg is above water. Write your measurement on the line.

_____

Tell how this measurement compares with your prediction.

_____

Draw a picture of your iceberg floating in the water. Write the measurements of the top section and the bottom section.

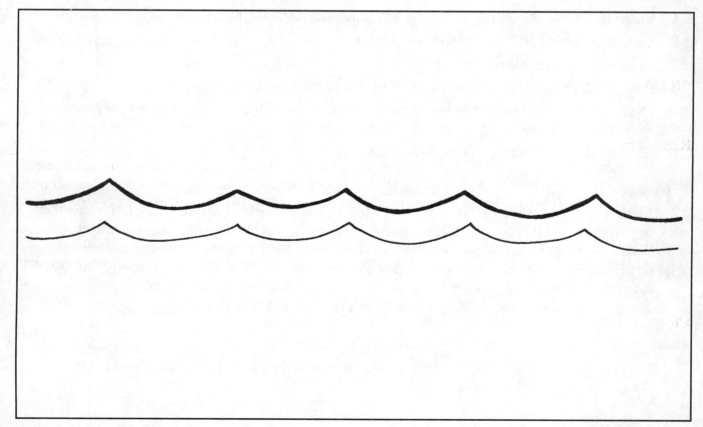

# Making a Mountain

## Question

How are mountains formed in the ocean?

## Setting the Stage

- Ask the students what they know about mountains. Record their responses on chart paper. Add to it throughout the lesson as new facts are learned. Establish that there are also underwater mountains.
- Review the layers of the earth's surface: the inner core, the outer core, the mantle, molten rock, and the crust. Make sure that the students understand that the area of molten fluid is under high pressure.

## Materials Needed for Each Individual

- clay or play dough in three different colors
- rolling pin (or other object to flatten the clay)
- wax paper
- data-capture sheet (page 46)

## Procedure *(Student Instructions)*

1. Spread a sheet of wax paper on a flat surface.
2. Roll each color clay into a thick rectangle. All three pieces should be the same size.
3. Cut two more pieces of wax paper. Place them on a flat surface so that they overlap one another about one inch in the center.
4. Stack the layers of clay onto the center of the papers as shown in the diagram.
5. Establish that the wax paper represents the earth's crust and molten layers; the clay layers are the mantle, outer core, and inner core.
6. Push the ends of the clay toward the middle until a mountain is formed.
7. Complete the data-capture sheet.

## Extensions

- The same movement that causes mountains can also cause earthquakes. Explore how earthquakes happen below the ocean. Find out the relationship of these earthquakes to the giant waves known as tsunamis. An excellent source of information for this project is *Giant Waves* by D.M. Souza (Carolrhoda Books, 1992).
- Learn about the theory of plate tectonics. Scientists believe that the earth's crust consists of several plates which float on the semi-molten rocks below. The continents sit on these plates and move along with the motion.

## Closure

In their ocean journals, have the students add a list of the layers of the earth and the composition (solid or liquid) of each one.

# Making a Mountain *(cont.)*

Explain what happened when you pushed the ends of the clay toward the middle.

_____

_____

_____

_____

_____

Draw a picture of your mountain in the space below.

On the back of this paper, draw a cross-section of the inside of the earth. Label these parts: the **inner core**, the **outer core**, the **mantle**, the **molten layer**, and the **crust**.

# Off the Richter Scale

## Question

What causes an underwater volcano to erupt?

## Setting the Stage

- Review the relationship between the molten layer below the earth's crust and earthquakes. Establish that the action of volcanoes is also related to the molten layer, but the result is different.
- Find Indonesia on a map or globe. Point out its island of Krakatoa. Explain to students that in 1883 Krakatoa was rocked by the eruption of its volcano. The noise from it could be heard thousands of miles away, even by people in Australia! Krakatoa's eruption triggered a tsunami which destroyed thousands of homes in Java and Sumatra; over 36,000 people drowned. Waves from the tsunami continued to circle the globe for days afterwards.

## Materials Needed for Each Group or the Class

- water
- skillet or pan
- metal funnel
- stove or hot plate
- data-capture sheet (page 48)

## Procedure *(Student Instructions)*

1. Place the funnel in the center of the skillet.
2. Pour enough water in the skillet to cover all but the top of the funnel's spout.
3. Place the water-filled skillet on the stove top and turn the setting to high.
4. Predict what will happen when the water begins to boil.
5. Observe what happens.
6. Complete the data-capture sheet.

## Extensions

- Read about the eruption of Mt. St. Helens in Washington in 1988. What were the effects of the volcano? Research more recent volcanic activity around the world. Find out how they impacted the environment.
- Read about underwater volcanoes in the book *Land Under the Sea* by Hershell H. Nixon and Joan Lowery Nixon (Dodd, Mead & Company, 1985).

## Closure

In their ocean journals, students can add a short summary of a newspaper or magazine article about a volcano eruption that occurred within the last 50 years.

# Off the Richter Scale *(cont.)*

| Prediction | Actual |
|---|---|
| Predict what will happen when the water begins to boil. | This is what happened when the water began to boil. |
| _____ _____ _____ _____ | _____ _____ _____ _____ |
| Draw a picture of what you think will happen. | Draw a picture of what actually happened. |

On the back of this sheet, draw a cross-section of a volcano. Label your picture with the **bolded** words in the paragraph below.

Below the earth's **crust** is a layer of molten rock. This hot, **molten rock** gives off **gases** and builds up pressure. When this pressure breaks through an opening in the crust, the **volcano** erupts. **Ash and cinders** are sent bursting into the air.

# Just the Facts

Think about this: Every day you come in contact with something that began in the ocean. In fact, we are dependent on the ocean for a number of things. On a sheet of paper, write or draw some ways in which we are dependent on the ocean. Compare your ideas with a partner. Look at the ways in which we depend on the ocean environment:

**FOOD:** An endless variety of fish is at our disposal, thanks to the ocean habitat. Fish, mussels, clams, oysters, crabs, lobsters, and shrimp supply us with important vitamins and nutrients. The ocean is also home to a number of edible plants such as seaweed, which is used in everything from hamburgers to ice cream.

**WATER CYCLE:** Ocean water is too salty to be used directly for drinking. Through the water cycle, however, ocean waters are evaporated by the sun and later returned to Earth as rain, which humans can drink.

**RESOURCES:** Hidden below the surface of the ocean is a vast array of products useful to man. The list includes such diverse resources as the fossil fuels, gas and oil; jewels and gemstones such as coral, mother-of-pearl, and tortoiseshell; metals including copper, nickel, and cobalt; sand, gravel, and other building materials; and sponges.

**TRANSPORTATION:** Although people mostly travel abroad in modern aircraft, some goods are more easily transported over the ocean waters. Cars, oil, foods, clothing, and decorative items are commonly exported and imported by huge freighters.

**MEDICINES AND RESEARCH:** Some ocean plants and animals are used to develop new medicines and vitamin supplements, including iodine and potassium. Scientists are also studying sharks, which have unusually hearty immune systems. It is hoped that these studies will lead to a cure for AIDS.

**WEATHER:** Ocean breezes bring warm and cool air to land masses. Their winds can also cause hurricanes and other fierce storms.

**FUN:** Playing on the beach is fun. You can build a sand castle, write your name in the sand, or bury your best friend. Fishing, surfing, boating, and swimming are just a few activities you can enjoy. Can you think of some more?

**BEAUTY:** Watch the waves as they come and go. Listen to the ocean's constant roar. Smell the salt in the air. Feel the damp, fresh ocean spray. The ocean is a beautiful and wondrous experience. It inspires us to create art, music, poetry, and great literature. Its seashells, pearls, and other precious jewels are worn by men and women alike.

All the secrets of the ocean are waiting for you to discover.

# Oil Spill

## Question

What are the effects of an oil spill on ocean waters?

## Setting the Stage

- One of the worst oil spills in the 20th century was the Exxon Valdez spill off the coast of Alaska. Find an article about the accident and read part of it to the class. Discuss the news story.
- With the students, discuss some other ways oceans can become polluted. Make a list of them on chart paper or the chalkboard.

## Materials Needed for Each Group

- stale popcorn (preferably unbuttered and unsalted; check with movie theaters for possible donations, or prepare your own with the class a few days prior to the experiment.)
- paper grocery bags
- stopwatch (or a watch with a second hand)
- clipboard, paper, and pencil
- small pond or lake
- data-capture sheet (page 51)

## Procedure *(Student Instructions)*

1. As a group choose a secretary, stopwatch controller, popcorn thrower, and observers.
2. For your group choose a location on the shore of the pond.
3. Fill your grocery bag with popcorn.
4. Predict how long it will take the popcorn to spread. Record the group's prediction on the data-capture sheet.
5. At a given signal, throw the popcorn into the water. At the same time, begin timing with the stopwatch. Record the time on the data-capture sheet.
6. Stop the watch when the popcorn spreads out.
7. The secretary records a statement from each observer explaining what the popcorn touches and attaches to and how it moved.

## Extensions

- Try different methods to contain the popcorn (oil) spill. Encourage students to create their own devices to clean up the spill. Back in the classroom, have the groups share their clean-up tools and explain how successful they were.
- To help students visualize an actual oil spill, have them mix some oil and water in a glass jar with a lid. Time them as they shake the jar. After one minute, observe what has happened. Continue to shake the jar for another minute. What happens now? Direct the students to find out what actually happens to the oil in an oil slick.

## Closure

In their ocean journals, have students add their impressions of a newspaper or magazine article they have read about a severe oil spill.

# Oil Spill *(cont.)*

**Directions:** Attach this page to a clipboard.  Choose a secretary to record all answers.

1. Group Prediction.  How long it will take the popcorn to spread? _____

   Actual time it took the popcorn to spread. _____

2. Describe how the popcorn spread.

   _____

   _____

3. What do you think helped the popcorn to spread?

   _____

   _____

4. What did the popcorn touch?

   _____

   _____

5. Where did most of the popcorn end up?  Why?

   _____

   _____

6. In the space below, draw a picture of a device or instrument that could be used to clean up the popcorn spill.

# Light As a Feather

## Question

How can heavy ships float?

## Setting the Stage

- Divide the students into small groups. Give each group a number of small objects such as a rock, ball of clay, pencil, plastic fork, small aluminum pie plate, etc. Each group will also need a Sink or Float chart (see page 53) and a pencil. Directions are on the page.
- With the class, discuss the following question: Does the shape or size of an object have anything to do with its ability to float? Establish that in order for something to float, the downward force of gravity on an object has to be balanced by the upward force of the water.
- Read *Archimedes' Bath* by Pamela Allen (Angus & Robertson, 1980) to the class. Tell the students they will be exploring a principle discovered by Archimedes.

## Materials Needed for Individual or Group

- a large piece of aluminum foil
- about one dozen paper clips
- clear plastic glass, 3/4 full of water
- data-capture sheet (page 54)

## Procedure *(Student Instructions)*

1. Fold the aluminum foil in half and bend it into the shape of a boat.
2. Place the boat on the water. If it does not float, reshape it until it floats right side up.
3. Put one paper clip in the boat. What happens? Add more clips, one at a time. How many paper clips can be added before the boat sinks? Record your guesses on the data-capture sheet.
4. Remove the boat and paper clips from the water.
5. Fold and flatten the foil boat over the paper clips so that they are enclosed.
6. Predict what will happen when you put the flattened boat back in the water. Observe.
7. Record your observations on the data-capture sheet.

## Extension

For homework have the students find three objects in their home that sink and three that float. After testing their theories, they can draw pictures of those objects in two columns on a folded sheet of paper—labeling one column FLOATS and the other column SINKS. Have the students share their homework with a partner or in a small group. Compile the completed projects in a special class folder.

## Closure

In their ocean journals, students can spread some liquid glue over a tiny area of the page, sprinkle with salt and then let it dry. Afterwards they can write a paragraph explaining how salt in the water helps keep things afloat.

# Light As a Feather (cont.)

## Sink or Float Chart

Choose a secretary to write the names of the objects and count the guesses.

- Write the name of each object in the middle column.
- Examine one object at a time. Decide if it will float or sink.
- Make a tally mark for each person's guess in the Guesses column.
- One at a time, place each object in the water.
- Did it float or sink? Mark the correct space in the Actual column.

| Guesses | | Object | Actual | |
|---|---|---|---|---|
| Float | Sink | | Float | Sink |
| | | | | |
| | | | | |
| | | | | |
| | | | | |
| | | | | |
| | | | | |
| | | | | |
| | | | | |
| | | | | |

# Light As a Feather *(cont.)*

Write each group member's name in a space along with their prediction of the highest number of paper clips the boat can hold before it sinks.

| | | | | | | |
|---|---|---|---|---|---|---|
| | | | | | | |

How many paper clips was the boat able to float? _____

Predict what will happen when the flattened boat is placed back in the water.

_____

_____

Explain what happened when the flattened boat was placed in the water.

_____

_____

Why was one boat able to float but not the other?

_____

_____

_____

Draw the shape of the boat that was able to float.

# Filter It Out

## Question

How does the ocean make water clean by filtering?

## Setting the Stage

- We often take clean water for granted. Ask the students what would happen if the water in their community became so polluted that they could not use it. Do they have any suggestions or methods for cleaning the water?
- Establish that the ocean is able to clean its own water through the process of filtering. Briefly discuss different types of filters (air conditioning, water, masks worn by painters, etc.)

## Materials Needed for Each Individual

- glass or plastic jar with lid
- soil (Get permission before digging up the ground!)
- pebbles or small rocks
- water
- data-capture sheet (page 56)

## Procedure *(Student Instructions)*

1. Fill the jar about 1/3 full of soil.
2. Add some pebbles or rocks.
3. Fill the jar not quite to the top with water.
4. Predict what will happen when you shake the jar.
5. Cover the jar tightly and shake. What happens to the water?
6. Allow the jar to stand for at least two days. What has happened to the water and the soil?
7. Draw a before and after picture on your data-capture sheet.

## Extensions

- Assign groups to create charts that show different ways to use water wisely.
- Make sure that students understand that water is purified naturally when particles settle to the bottom of the ocean or a river or lake.
- Read *The Magic School Bus at the Waterworks* by Joanna Cole (Scholastic, 1986).

## Closure

In their ocean journals, have the students draw a chart of some ways they can use water wisely.

# Filter It Out *(cont.)*

1. Predict what will happen when you shake the jar. _____

_____

_____

2. Observation—Day 1: _____

_____

3. Observation—Day 2: _____

_____

4. Results of the Experiment: _____

_____

In the space below, draw a before and after picture of the contents of the jar.

| **Before** | **After** |
|---|---|
| | |

# Microscopic Food

**Question**

How does the sun feed ocean animals?

**Setting the Stage**

- With the class, brainstorm a list of ways that man is dependent on the ocean. Establish that one reason people depend on the ocean is for the food it provides. The experiment they will be doing will show the relationship between the sun and food from the ocean.
- Review or introduce the food chain to students. Draw a diagram of the food chain on the chalkboard or chart paper.
- Ask students what would happen if plants did not get any sun. Explain that creatures are also dependent on the sun.

**Materials Needed for Each Individual Student or Group**

- two same size, same variety plants
- masking tape
- marking pen
- shoe box
- tap water
- data-capture sheet (page 58)

**Procedure** (*Student Instructions*)

1. With the marking pen, write your name on two pieces of masking tape.
2. Label each plant with your name.
3. Place one plant where there is a source of sunlight.
4. Place the other plant in a shoe box. Keep it covered.
5. Water both plants as normal.
6. Observe the plants over a period of five days.
7. Record your observations on the data-capture sheet.

**Extensions**

- If possible, examine some ocean water for plankton under a microscope. If ocean water is not available, use pond or river water. Have the students draw a picture of what they see.
- Draw a food chain poster to show how large fish eat smaller fish, which eat tiny water animals, which eat plankton.
- Where and how in the human food chain does seafood fit in? Divide a round paper plate into fourths. Write a different stage of the food chain in each section. Cut out a 1/4 section from another paper plate. Place it on top of the other plate. Push a brad through the center of both plates. Turn the bottom plate to reveal one step of the food chain at a time.

**Closure**

In their ocean journals, have the students write the journey of a microscopic plant plankton as it makes its way through the ocean food chain.

# Microscopic Food *(cont.)*

**Directions:** Write your daily observations of the plants in the chart below.

|  | **Plant 1** | **Plant 2** |
|---|---|---|
| **Day 1** | | |
| **Day 2** | | |
| **Day 3** | | |
| **Day 4** | | |
| **Day 5** | | |

On the back of this paper, tell which plant grew better and explain why.

# Seaweed for Lunch

**Question**

How much of our daily food comes from seaweed?

**Setting the Stage**

- Bring in a label from a canned or frozen food. Write the names of all the ingredients on the chalkboard or overhead projector as a student reads them aloud. Examine the list of ingredients and identify additives such as preservatives, vitamins, and minerals. Are the students familiar with any of them? Discuss why these ingredients are added to foods.

- Ask the students for a show of hands to indicate how many of them have ever eaten seaweed. Tell them that most likely they all have eaten seaweed at one time or another but that they may not have been aware of it. This experiment will show them how seaweed fits into their diets.

**Materials Needed for Each Individual**

- pencil
- food labels from home pantry and refrigerators/freezers
- data-capture sheet (page 60)
- **Note:** If not enough home products contain seaweed, it may be necessary to check supermarket shelves to conduct this experiment.

**Procedure** (*Student Instructions*)

1. Take home your data-capture sheet.
2. Get permission to go through the pantry and refrigerator/freezer in your home. Be sure to put things back where you found them!
3. Examine the labels on all the food items you can find, including spices, canned, and packaged foods.
4. In the ingredients' listings, look for any of the following words: carrageenin, agar, algin, alginates, and chondrus. These indicate that seaweed is one of the ingredients in that product.
5. On your data-capture sheet, write the names of the products that contain seaweed.
6. Compare your results with a partner.

**Extensions**

- Divide the students into groups. Have them make a graph using the information gathered from their data-capture sheets.
- In class make a seaweed dish. Recipes for seaweed cooking can be found in the book *The Seavegetable Book: Foraging and Cooking Seaweed* by J.C. Madlener (Clarkson N. Potter, 1977).
- Carrageenin and other seaweed extracts are also used in nonfood products such as shampoo, soap, shoe polish, chewing gum, paint, and toothpaste. Direct the students to examine the labels of some of these products in their homes. Does their toothpaste contain seaweed?

**Closure**

Tell the students to make a list in their ocean journals of all the food and nonfood products they found that contain some form of seaweed.

# Seaweed for Lunch *(cont.)*

**Directions:** In each space below, write the names of the food products you can find that contain the listed ingredients.  Then compare your data with a partner.

## Food Products

| | |
|---|---|
| **carrageenin** | |
| **agar** | |
| **algin** | |
| **alginates** | |
| **chondrus** | |

Which of the five ingredients above did you find the most often?

_____

Which of these food items do you eat the most?

_____

What food items did you and your partner have in common?

_____

_____

_____

# Temperatures

## Question

How does the ocean affect the temperature of land?

## Setting the Stage

- Compare the winter and summer temperatures of land areas close to the ocean with land areas far from the effects of the ocean.
- Fill two same-size glasses with the same amount of water. Place one in direct sunlight and the other in a shaded area. Put a thermometer in each glass. After about 20 minutes, read the thermometers in each glass. In which glass is the temperature higher? What does this tell us about ocean water?

## Materials Needed for Each Group or the Whole Class

- baking pan, about 2" (5 cm) deep
- thermometer
- large ball of clay or play dough
- water
- electric fan
- data-capture sheet (page 62)

## Procedure *(Student Instructions)*

1. Fill the baking pan almost to the top with water.
2. Place the pan of water flat in the center of a table.
3. Mold the clay so that when the thermometer is positioned in the clay, it will be about 12" (30 cm) above the table (see diagram).
4. Place the thermometer 12" (30 cm) from one end of the pan.
5. At the opposite end of the pan position the fan so that it is about 12" (30 cm) from the pan. WARNING: Do not allow the fan to make contact with the water!
6. Turn the fan on a moderate setting. On the data-capture sheet, record changes in the temperature.
7. Try a different fan setting to see what happens.
8. Predict what will happen when the fan is turned off. Record the results.

## Extensions

- Continue to investigate how the ocean affects land temperatures. Make sure that students understand that during the day, land near the ocean warms the air above it and draws in cooler air from the ocean. At night, air above the ocean (which is now warm from absorbing the sun's energy all day) rises and draws the cooler air from the land.
- Learn about the two great wind systems that move the surface water of the ocean—the Trade Winds and the Westerlies. Tell how and where they move.

## Closure

In their ocean journals, have the students write a paragraph explaining how the ocean affects the temperature of land.

# Temperatures *(cont.)*

On the chart below record the beginning temperature in the bottom space.
Record the temperature every minute for five minutes.

| |
|---|
| |
| |
| |
| |
| |
| |

Temperature after five minutes

Temperature after four minutes

Temperature after three minutes

Temperature after two minutes

Temperature after one minute

Beginning Temperature

Where did the biggest temperature change occur? _____

Why? _____

_____

When did the temperature begin to stay the same? _____

_____

Turn the fan setting on higher.  What happens to the temperature now?

_____

Predict what will happen when you turn the fan off. _____

_____

Turn off the fan.  Wait a few minutes and record what happens._____

_____

_____

_____

_____

_____

_____

62

# Sandy Glass

**Question**

How can sand be used to make glass?

**Setting the Stage**

- Ask the students if they know how glass is made. Establish that glass is mostly sand that has been melted in a large furnace.
- Make a list of the different uses of glass—windows, sunglasses, drinking glasses, neon lights, car windows, etc. Are they all constructed the same way?

**Materials Needed for Each Group**

- cooking oil
- aluminum pie pan
- hot plate
- heavy sauce pan with lid
- 1/2 cup (125 mL) of water
- 1 cup (250 mL) of granulated sugar

- 5 tablespoons (75 mL) of light corn syrup
- wooden spoon
- candy thermometer or a glass of ice water
- oven mitt
- refrigerator
- data-capture sheet (page 64)

**Procedure** *(Student Instructions)*

1. Lightly oil the bottom and sides of the aluminum pan. Set aside.
2. Place the pan on the hot plate and then pour the water into the pan.
3. Add the sugar and then stir with the wooden spoon.
4. Add the corn syrup and stir.
5. Turn the hot plate setting to high.
6. Cover the pan and bring the mixture to a boil.
7. Uncover the pan and without stirring, keep boiling the mixture until it reaches 310° F. (154° C). **Note:** If you do not have a candy thermometer, add one drop of the mixture to the ice water. When the drop forms a fine, clear thread, it is hot enough.
8. Remove from the heat immediately—too much cooking will cause it to turn brown—and pour evenly into the prepared pan. WARNING: Do not touch the mixture because it is extremely hot and may cause burns!
9. Cool the pan in the refrigerator for at least 30 minutes.
10. Remove the "glass" from the pan. Observe its characteristics.
11. Complete the data-capture sheet.

**Extensions**

- Mirrors are made from glass. Experiment with mirrors to find out how they bend, reflect, and refract light.
- For more information about glassmaking, read *From Sand to Glass* by Ali Mitgutsch (Carolrhoda, 1981) or *Glass* by Susan Cackett (Gloucester Press, 1988).

**Closure**

In their ocean journals, have the students write a story that tells how important glass is in their daily lives.

# Sandy Glass *(cont.)*

**Directions:** Circle Yes or No after each question.

1. Before you add the sugar to the water, look at it. Is it clear?

   YES                    NO

2. After you added the sugar to the water, did it look clear?

   YES                    NO

3. After you added the corn syrup to the sugar/water mixture did it look clear?

   YES                    NO

4. When the mixture began to boil, did it look clear?

   YES                    NO

5. When the mixture cooled, did it look clear?

   YES                    NO

6. What happened when the sugar was heated? (Circle all that apply.)

   It melted.          It fused.          It turned brown.          It stayed clear.

7. How did the surface of the cooled mixture look? (Circle all that apply.)

   It was opaque.          It was clear.          It was shiny.          It was smooth.

8. When heated, sand changes in the same way as the sugar/water/syrup mixture did. Tell what happens to sand when it melts and fuses.

   _____

   _____

   _____

   _____

9. The result of this experiment is what is known as breakaway glass. It is used for stunts in movies. Explain why it is used in place of real glass.

   _____

   _____

   _____

64

# Resource Removal

## Question

How are some resources removed from the ocean?

## Setting the Stage

Make a list of some ocean resources. Discuss some of the methods in which they are gathered from the ocean—fishing, mining, diving, pumps, etc.

## Materials Needed for Each Group

- eyedropper or turkey baster
- clear empty sprayer from a spray bottle
- pan of water
- data-capture sheet (page 66)

## Procedure *(Student Instructions)*

1. Keeping the bulb of the eyedropper or turkey baster above water level, suck some water into the tube.
2. Squirt the water back out. What do you observe?
3. Record your observations on the data-capture sheet.
4. Now submerge the eyedropper or turkey baster in the pan of water.
5. Suck up some water and try squirting it back out under the water.
6. Record your observations on the data-capture sheet.
7. Place the tube end of the sprayer into the water.
8. Pump the handle until water sprays out.
9. On your data-capture sheet compare the action of the sprayer with the pumping action of the eyedropper or turkey baster.

## Extensions

- Demonstrate another method of water movement—capillary action. Cut a strip of paper towel, and put a piece of tape on one end. Place the opposite end of the towel into a cup of water, which has been placed next to a wall. Press the tape onto the wall to hold up the paper towel strip. Predict what will happen. Observe.
- Challenge students to move water from a full cup to an empty one. (This process is called siphoning.) Each group of students will need one plastic cup filled with water, one empty plastic cup, a piece of flexible plastic tubing about 3' (1 m) long and 1/2" (1.25 cm) thick, and water. Place the full cup higher than the empty cup. Put one end of the tube into the full cup (so that the tube touches the cup's bottom), and bend it down into the empty cup.

## Closure

In their ocean journals, have the students draw a picture of a squirt gun and explain how it works.

# Resource Removal *(cont.)*

1. **Above Water Level**

   What happened when you compressed the bulb? _____

   _____

   What happened when you tried to squirt the water back out? _____

   _____

2. **Below Water Level**

   What happened when you compressed the bulb? _____

   _____

   What happened when you squirted the water back out? _____

   _____

In the chart below compare the action of the eyedropper or baster with the action of the sprayer.

| Eyedropper | Sprayer |
|------------|---------|
|            |         |

66

# She Sells Seashells

## Question

Can seashells bring beauty into our lives?

## Setting the Stage

- Discuss with the class some ways in which ocean treasures can bring beauty into their lives. For example, they can be worn as jewelry, used to adorn picture frames, or displayed in glass jars for all to view.
- Briefly discuss where seashells come from. Identify some shells and the animals that previously lived in them.
- If possible, go on a class field trip. Look for and identify different types of shells.

## Materials Needed for Each Group

- 4 different shells in a variety of colors, shapes, and sizes (It is suggested that you use any of these types in order to provide a good variety: a conch shell large enough so that it can be held up to the ear; a barnacle; a clam shell; abalone; a whelk; and a boring turret snail.)
- a pencil
- data-capture sheet (page 68)

## Procedure (*Student Instructions*)

1. Explore the shells using all of your senses—sight, touch, smell, and hearing.
2. Draw a picture of each shell, and record your observations of them on the data-capture sheet.
3. Share your observations with the rest of the group.

## Extensions

- Start a class shell collection. Attach each shell to a sheet of heavy cardboard. Below each shell, write its common name, its scientific name, and the locations where it is commonly found.
- Make a list of edible shellfish. Ask students which kind of shellfish is their favorite. Have them make a graph of the results.
- In some cultures, shells were used as money. Find out about some of these cultures. Are there any cultures that still use shells for money?
- Gather a variety of shells. Have the students compare their lengths, colors, shapes, and any patterns they may have.

## Closure

In their ocean journals, have the students draw and color a picture of their favorite kind of shell. Tell them to write a haiku poem to explain what the shell means to them.

# She Sells Seashells *(cont.)*

**Directions:** In each box draw a picture of a seashell. Write words or phrases to describe each one's shape, color, texture, and other characteristics.

| | |
|---|---|
| **Shell #1**<br><br><br><br>Shape: _____<br><br>Color: _____<br><br>Texture: _____<br><br>Other: _____ | **Shell #2**<br><br><br><br>Shape: _____<br><br>Color: _____<br><br>Texture: _____<br><br>Other: _____ |
| **Shell #3**<br><br><br><br>Shape: _____<br><br>Color: _____<br><br>Texture: _____<br><br>Other: _____ | **Shell #4**<br><br><br><br>Shape: _____<br><br>Color: _____<br><br>Texture: _____<br><br>Other: _____ |

Which shell is your favorite? Why? _____

_____

# Language Arts

Science is the systematic study of natural phenomena. It requires the use of higher-level thinking skills, such as observing, questioning, predicting, categorizing, and hypothesizing. These skills do not stand alone, however. They also depend on knowledge learned in other areas of the curriculum. For example, students must know how to construct charts—a math concept—or how to write a hypothesis—a language arts skill. Directly or indirectly, many areas of the curriculum are naturally interconnected. On this and the following "Curriculum Connections" pages, you will be given a number of ways to further these connections.

Beginning with language arts there are numerous literature selections for you to choose from. Check the Bibliography on pages 95 and 96 of this book to help you get started. After determining a science concept as your focus, plan your lessons to reflect that concept. Some examples follow.

**SCIENCE CONCEPT:** *The ocean has many purposes.*

*I Am the Ocean* by Suzanna Marshak (Arcade Publishing, 1991).

A simply-written and beautifully-illustrated ode to the ocean and all that it contains.

- Make a web of all the things that are in the ocean.
- Have the students explain how waves are formed. Dicsuss how waves impact everything in and on the ocean.
- Make a list of all the animals that live in the ocean or that depend on the ocean.
- Draw an ocean food chain.
- Explain the role of the ocean in the hydrologic cycle. Draw a picture of this cycle.
- Find out how tides are caused.
- Write a poem or haiku about the ocean.

**SCIENCE CONCEPT:** *The ocean is composed of various layers.*

*What's Under the Sea?* by Nancy Gugelman Johnstone (Abingdon Press, 1992).

This book introduces the reader to the various layers of the ocean and tells how we find out about them.

- Draw pictures of the different land features found on the ocean floor. Tell how they were formed.
- Draw a floor plan of the ocean floor. Compare these drawings to actual maps of the ocean floor or diagrams found in science books.
- Discuss how earthquakes and volcanoes can happen in the ocean. What effects can undersea earthquakes and volcanoes have on the rest of the world?
- Discuss some ways that man is able to explore the ocean floor. Find out how submersibles enable man to reach the ocean bottom.
- Read about some pioneers of underwater exploration. Write a report about one of those pioneers.

# Language Arts *(cont.)*

**SCIENCE CONCEPT:** *Communities store water in reservoirs and clean the water through a purification process.*

*The Magic School Bus at the Waterworks* by Joanna Cole (Scholastic, Inc, 1986).

- Pre-Reading Activity: Discuss with the class how impurities get into our water and how they think these impurities are removed.

- Have each child draw a diagram of the water cycle. Follow up with a written assignment: For example, tell the students to pretend they are a droplet of water, and write about their adventures as they go through the water cycle.

- After reading the story, direct the students to write 10 facts they have learned about water.

- Write a story telling how water systems become polluted in the first place. Discuss what can be done to prevent pollution.

- Divide the students into groups. Have each group make a chart of some things they can do to help save water.

- As a follow-up to the preceeding activity, have the students write a conversation they might have with an adult to convince them that they, too, should help conserve water.

- In their own words, have the students explain how a cloud is formed. Extend this activity and assign the class to draw pictures of the different types of clouds (cumulus, nimbus, cirrus, stratus, etc.).

- Write a play in which the characters—water droplets—are purified. Action can begin at the reservoir and end with the water mains that enter buildings.

- Construct flow charts that show how water is purified. As an alternate activity, give each group of students a number of large index cards or sheets of construction paper. On each page write a different step in the water purification process. Then draw a picture to illustrate each one.

- Plan a class field trip to your community's waterworks, or invite one of their representatives to speak to your class. Beforehand, guide the students to write a number of questions they want to ask the guest speaker. Have them write their questions on separate index cards. Review them to make sure there are no duplicates.

- Conduct a class debate about rationing water to homes and businesses as a way to cut down on water usage, or let the students determine a water-related topic they would like to discuss.

- As a culminating activity, build a water-purification system. Directions for one can be found on page 71.

# Language Arts *(cont.)*

## Culminating Activity—Water Purification System

**Materials Needed for Each Group or Individual**

- an old glass
- sieve
- bowl
- scissors (or knife)
- plastic bottle
- cotton puffs or cotton batting
- water mixed with soil, sand, and leaves
- sand
- gravel
- blotting paper
- measuring cups

**Procedure** *(Student Instructions)*

1. With the scissors, cut off the bottom of a plastic bottle.

2. Stuff some cotton into the neck of the bottle, as shown in the diagram.

3. Pour the water mixed with soil, sand, and leaves through the sieve into a bowl. Reserve the water in a large measuring cup.

4. Record the amount of water in the cup.

5. Turn the plastic bottle upside down over the glass (as shown).

6. Layer the remaining materials, and pour the dirty water into the filter. Observe.

7. Measure the amount of liquid recovered. Compare that with the amount originally poured into the system. Discuss what happened to the rest of the water.

8. Let the students determine how they will present their data. Have each group create its own data-capture sheet.

**Closure**

Instruct the students to write step-by-step instructions for performing this experiment.

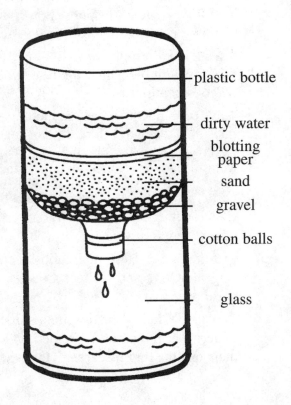

plastic bottle

dirty water

blotting paper

sand

gravel

cotton balls

glass

# Language Arts *(cont.)*

Here are some more ideas to help you connect language arts with science.

- Assign students to read a story about the ocean. Afterwards have them write a list of at least five things the story taught them about the ocean.
- Read aloud a story or poem about the sea. Some appropriate titles can be found in the box below.

---

**Suggested Literature**

*At the Beach* by Anne Rockwell (Macmillan, 1987).

*At the Seaside* by Robert Lewis Stevenson from *A Child's Garden of Verses* (Chronicle Books, 1989).

*Beaches* and *Sitting in the Sand* by Karla Kuskin from *Dogs & Dragons, Trees & Dreams* (Harper Trophy, 1992).

*Famous Seaweed Soup* by Antoinette Truglio Martin (Alberg Whitman &Co., 1993).

*The Little Mermaid* by Hans Christian Andersen, retold by Deborah Hautzig (Random House, 1987). A Step into Reading book.

*The Sea Gypsy* by Richard Hovey from *Piping Down the Valleys Wild* (Dell Publishing, 1968).

*The Sea Is Calling Me* by Lee Bennett Hopkins (Harcourt Brace Jovanovich, 1986), Poetry collection.

*Until I Saw the Sea* by Lilian Moore from *Sing a Song of Popcorn* (Scholastic, 1988).

---

- Ask the students what questions they have about the ocean and what they would like to know about it. Write all responses on chart paper with the same color marking pen or crayon. Save the chart for later reference.
- Assign small groups or individuals to explore each question. Let them determine how they will proceed with their investigation, what materials they will use, and how they will record any data and observations.
- After the students have conducted their experiments, review the chart. Add answers to their questions using a different color marking pen or crayons.
- Have the students write their own stories or poems based on their questions about the ocean.
- Read paragraphs or selected excerpts from magazine articles to spark student interest in a particular topic. A number of excellent science-related magazines are currently on the market. Check with your school librarian or local library for *National Geographic World*, *Owl*, *Chickadee*, *Ranger Rick*, or *3-2-1-Contact*.
- List the names of some famous oceanologists on the chalkboard. Some names to include are Eugenie Clark and Jacques Cousteau. Assign students to read biographies on these or other ocean scientists.
- Groups of students can write a skit or play about a giant wave that destroyed a village or how an underwater mountain is formed or some other concept based on what they have learned through their reading and research. Have them present their play to the rest of the class.

# Social Studies

The ocean is an integral part of the world's history and cultures. Without it there would be no life as we know it. For centuries people have depended on the ocean for basic needs such as food and water. Today those same needs (and more) continue to be met by the gifts offered by earth's largest water resource.

Because of man's dependence on the ocean for so many aspects of life, it is easy to connect science with social studies. Whether you are emphasizing history, geography, or cultural awareness, you can incorporate science concepts in the social studies curriculum. Some examples follow.

**SCIENCE CONCEPT**: *People the world over are dependent on the ocean.*

- Divide the students into groups. Give them 10 minutes to list all the edible ocean products that they can think of. Compare the lists as a whole group. What are some by-products made from them?

- Examine how fish are prepared and eaten in various cultures. Which countries eat the most seafood? Make a graph of the results. Discuss why the students think some countries consume more fish than others.

- Discuss some other foods we get from the ocean. Learn how seaweed has become an important ingredient in many of our foods. Have students examine food labels for carageenan or algin, both of which are ocean plants used as preservatives.

- What are some other products besides food that we get from the ocean? Learn how medicines such as iodine and cod liver oil are derived from the ocean. Find out how some fertilizer is made from certain kinds of seaweeds.

- Many people have careers that involve the ocean. There are divers, commercial fishermen, offshore drillers, marine biologists, marine geologists, aquaculturists, ichthyologists, and oceanographers, just to name a few. Have each student choose one career they might be interested in and find out about the duties it entails and the opportunities available.

- The ocean provides a means of transportation between countries. Have the students find out the different types of cargo transported by ocean liners. Discuss why all goods are not shipped by air. Talk about why ocean transportation is still an important means of importing and exporting goods.

- In conjunction with the previous project, study the different types of sailing vessels used through the ages. How have they changed through the centuries? What advances in instrumentation have been made? Make actual models of some old ships, or draw pictures of some and label their parts.

# Social Studies *(cont.)*

- People depend on the ocean for many enjoyments from surfing to swimming to skiing to just plain watching the waves. Have the students find out about other types of water activities (triathlons, wind surfing, boating, cruises, etc.).

- Many beautiful objects come from the ocean. Pearls and seashells are among the most commonly used items. Bring in a collection of seashells. Have the students classify them by type; sort them by size, shape, or color; or identify them by their scientific names. Learn how natural pearls are formed. Find out about the process of making cultured pearls.

- Find out how the ocean contributes to the economy in some communities. Look at topics such as tourism, commercial fishing, and retail sales of work and sports-related equipment.

- Discuss with the class the effects of pollution on the ocean. How, in turn, does that affect the food supply? Find out what, if anything, is currently being done to address the problem.

- Take a look at the geography of the ocean. What land forms are hidden beneath the waters? How do these land forms compare to those on dry ground? Draw pictures or diagrams of mountains, valleys, plateaus, and trenches. Learn how these various land forms are created. Compare the deepest and tallest parts of the ocean with the deepest and tallest parts of the land. Name them and find them on a map.

- Learn about some cultures that depend entirely or almost entirely on the ocean for their food, clothing, shelter, and economy in general. Compare their way of life with a culture that is not so dependent on the ocean.

- Find out how the weather is affected by the ocean. What countries might be more affected than others? Why?

- Discuss the role of the ocean in the history of exploration. What were some early fears and misconceptions about the ocean? Who were some of the early explorers, and how far were their journeys? What kind of scientific instruments did they use on their trips?

- The ocean is full of hidden treasures from sunken ships. They provide us with valuable information about life long ago and also contain some important artifacts. Students will enjoy reading about these adventures. Recommended books include the following:

    *The Atocha Treasure* by Sara Gennings (Rourke, 1988).

    *Exploring the Titanic* by Robert D. Ballard (Scholastic, 1988).

    *Sunken Treasure* by Gail Gibbons (Harper Collins, 1988).

    *The Titanic Lost . . .And Found* by Judy Donnelly (Random House, 1987). A Step Into Reading book.

# Physical Education

Watch the ocean for even a moment and what you see is a graceful, ever-moving organism. One way to convey this concept is through a physical approach to science. Teach your students about the rhythm and beauty of the ocean through movements which reflect their knowledge of the ocean.

The ocean is also a source of nutrition for the human body. Tie in concepts of nutrition with knowledge about ocean plants and creatures. Here are some examples to help you get started.

**SCIENCE CONCEPT:** *Ocean waters are constantly in motion.*

- Have the students pretend they are a bath toy adrift at sea. Tell them to move as if they were on top of a wave. Have them show how they would move if the wind started to blow and was causing even bigger waves.

- A parachute is an excellent means of exploring wave action. Let the students experiment with small ripples and gradually increase to larger and larger ones.

- With a parachute play a game of Tsunami. Tell the students to count off by fours and to remember their number. Students should stand evenly spaced around the parachute. Have them begin to make waves. When you yell "Tsunami!" everyone should lift the chute at once. Then quickly announce a number from one to four. If you say three, for example, all the threes must race from their space to the opposite side of the parachute before it lands on them. Continue in this manner until all numbers have had a chance to cross to the other side.

- Tell the students to pretend they are fish that live in the ocean. Divide them into groups and have them move around in schools of fish with one person in each group as the leader.

- Play a game of Follow the Leader. Choose one person to be the lead fish. Encourage them to make up movements that simulate fish swimming in the ocean.

**SCIENCE CONCEPT:** *The ocean provides us with much-needed nutrients.*

- Discuss nutrients and their importance to our nutrition. What are some nutrients provided by various seafoods?

- Display a copy of the food pyramid. Where is seafood on the diagram? Why? How important is fish in our diets?

- Have a tasting party. Supply a number of fish products and other seafoods such as clam juice, fish sticks, sushi, calamari, etc. Make a graph of the class favorites.

- Find out the nutritional content of some fish meals at fast food restaurants. Compare the findings. What effect does frying the fish have on its nutritional value?

# Math

Math connects readily with the study of oceans. Students will use their counting, graphing, measuring, and comparing skills during the course of their ocean studies. Here are some ways that these and other math skills can be incorporated into your ocean lessons.

- Display pre-made graphs, charts, and tables. For example, some newspapers and calendars provide tables which show times for high and low tides. Share these with the students and show them how to read the information provided. Model with the students how to make their own charts and graphs based on data they have collected.

- Provide a number of measuring instruments when doing the experiments. For example, you may supply measuring cups and spoons, meter sticks, or rulers with both metric and standard measurements. Review or teach the students how to use these tools.

- Compare results among groups. To show students how to read and interpret information in charts and graphs. Ask questions such as: Who had the most? The least? What is the difference between?

- After the students are familiar and comfortable with data collecting, encourage them to create their own ways to record information.

- Using the same data, show the students how to construct different types of graphs, such as a pie graph, line graph, bar graph, and picture graph. Tell the students to look for examples of these different types of graphs in all of the materials they read for research and information (trade books, magazines, newspapers, etc.).

- Extend the use of student-constructed graphs. Tell the students to make summary statements about the data. For example, more of the animals surveyed were mollusks than crustaceans. Another math activity to do with data on a graph is to convert the figures to percentages or fractions. Ask, for example: What fraction of the animals were mollusks? What percentage of the animals were crustaceans?

**SCIENCE CONCEPT**: *There are many geometric shapes which appear naturally in the ocean.*

- Divide the students into pairs or groups. Have them look through books about the ocean or science magazines to find examples of geometric shapes. After an allotted amount of time have the pairs or groups exchange their findings with another pair or group.

- Choose one shape— for example, a pentagon. What sea creatures have five appendages? On a large sheet of poster board have each student add his/her picture of a creature with five parts. Label the top of the poster with an appropriate title such as Ocean Pentagons.

- Give each pair or group of students a handful of shells. What geometric shapes can the students find among the shells, or what geometric shapes can they make using the shells?

# Art

The ocean is at once powerful and beautiful, commanding the respect and awe of all who view it. Over the centuries the ocean has inspired many people to create art which expresses their appreciation for the wonder of this vast body of water. Connecting art with science is a natural, and some ideas are presented below.

- Examine the work of some famous artists. How did they depict the ocean in their art? Have the students draw ocean pictures using the same style as a particular artist. Some paintings to look for include: *Improvisation 31 (Sea Battle)* by Wassily Kandinsky; *Beasts of the Sea* by Henri Matisse; *Sloop Nassau* by Winslow Homer; and *Sinbad the Sailor* by Paul Klee. (For more on this art topic see Teacher Created Materials #494 *Focus on Artists*.)

- Learn how pearls and seashells are used to make jewelry and objects of art. Students can make their own seashell jewelry. With a straight pin carefully poke a hole through the top of each shell. Thread a needle with gold thread or crochet thread, and sew enough shells to make a bracelet or necklace.

- Look for examples of the influence of shells and other ocean artifacts on objects in everyday life, such as clothing, pictures, wallpaper, pottery designs, etc.

- Some colors are named after things found in the ocean. Have the students look for examples of these colors in their homes, at stores, and in product catalogs: periwinkle, coral, abalone, and sand.

**SCIENCE CONCEPT**: *Tides wash up algae and other materials on the shore.*

**Materials Needed for Each Individual**

- algae washed up on shore
- pan of water
- newspapers
- sheet of construction paper
- wax paper
- stack of books or other heavy objects
- colored plastic wrap
- clear tape

**Procedure** (*Student Instructions*)

1. Cover the area with newspaper.
2. If the algae is dry, soak it in some water for a few minutes.
3. Remove the algae from the water and arrange it on the construction paper.
4. Cut two sheets of wax paper and sandwich the algae arrangement between them.
5. Place the stack of books on top of the papers, and allow to dry at least two days.
6. Remove the wax paper. Cover the algae with colored plastic wrap, and tape it down on the back of the paper.

# Observe

Before beginning your investigation, write your group members' names by their jobs below.

_____Team Leader          _____Stenographer

_____Oceanographer          _____Transcriber

Use all of your senses to gather information about these ocean products. Record your observations on the chart below. When you have finished your chart, as a group choose any two of the ocean products. On the back of this page, draw a picture of each one. Then make a chart to show how these two products are alike and how they are different.

| Product | Pearl | Kelp | Salt | Seashell |
|---------|-------|------|------|----------|
| **shape** | | | | |
| **color** | | | | |
| **smell** | | | | |
| **taste** | | | | |
| **texture** | | | | |

Put your finished activity paper in the collection pocket on the side of the table at this station.

# Communicate

Before beginning your investigation, write your group members' names by their jobs below.

_____Team Leader          _____Stenographer

_____Oceanographer        _____Transcriber

At this station you will find eight items to use to make a bar graph. Your completed bar graph will show at a glance how many plant, animal, and non-living ocean resources you have grouped together.

- Sort the items into three groups: plants, animals, or nonliving.
- Decide on a different color to represent each group. Fill in the Color Key below the bar graph.
- Count the number of plants, animals, and nonliving ocean resources. Color in the correct number of spaces on the graph.

| | Plant | Animal | Nonliving |
|---|---|---|---|
| 5 | | | |
| 4 | | | |
| 3 | | | |
| 2 | | | |
| 1 | | | |

## Color Key

Plant  =  [        ]                    Nonliving = [        ]

Animal = [        ]

On the back of this activity paper, make a circle graph of the eight plant, animal, and nonliving ocean resources at this table.

Put your finished activity paper in the collection pocket on the side of the table at this station.

# Compare

Before beginning your investigation, write your group members' names by their jobs below.

_____Team Leader        _____Stenographer

_____Oceanographer        _____Transcriber

There are three jars of water at this station: one is regular tap water, one is filtered tap water, and the third is purified, bottled water. Examine each type—look at it, smell it, pour some out. Then take a taste of each one and compare them. Write your comments in the spaces below. Vote for your favorite, and mark tallies in each column.

|  | Tap Water | Filtered Water | Purified Water |
|---|---|---|---|
| **Looks:** | | | |
| **Smells:** | | | |
| **Pours:** | | | |
| **Tastes:** | | | |
| **Favorite:** | | | |

On the back of this activity sheet, make a graph of the group's favorite type of water.

Put your finished activity paper in the collection pocket on the side of the table at this station.

# Order

Before beginning your investigation, write your group members' names by their jobs below.

_____Team Leader            _____Stenographer

_____Oceanographer         _____Transcriber

At this table you will find five different shells. Arrange them by size from smallest to largest. Draw a picture of them in the order you have made. Next, arrange them by weight from lightest to heaviest. Draw a picture of them in the order you have made. Third, arrange them by texture from smoothest to roughest. Draw a picture of them in the order you have made.

**Smallest to Largest**
**1 – 2– 3 – 4 – 5**

|  |  |  |  |  |
|--|--|--|--|--|
|  |  |  |  |  |

**Lightest to Heaviest**
**1 – 2– 3 – 4 – 5**

|  |  |  |  |  |
|--|--|--|--|--|
|  |  |  |  |  |

**Smoothest to Roughest**
**1 – 2– 3 – 4 – 5**

|  |  |  |  |  |
|--|--|--|--|--|
|  |  |  |  |  |

On the back of this activity page, arrange the shells by color from lightest to darkest or think of another way you can order them. Be sure to draw pictures, and number them in the order you have chosen.

Put your finished activity paper in the collection pocket on the side of the table at this station.

# Categorize

Before beginning your investigation, write your group members' names by their jobs below.

_____Team Leader     _____Stenographer

_____Oceanographer     _____Transcriber

On the table you will find labeled pictures of a variety of ocean resources. Categorize and write the names in the proper sections of the chart below. Some names may fit in more than one category.

| Uses | Ocean Resources |
|------|-----------------|
| **Fertilizer** | |
| **Food** | |
| **Building Materials** | |
| **Fuel** | |
| **Jewelry** | |
| **Making Glass** | |
| **Medicine** | |
| **Decorative and Art Objects** | |
| **Vitamins and Minerals** | |

On the back of this activity paper, make a group chart that shows another way to categorize the ocean resources found on this table.

Put your finished activity paper in the collection pocket on the side of the table at this station.

# Relate

Before beginning your investigation, write your group members' names by their jobs below.

_____Team Leader          _____Stenographer

_____Oceanographer        _____Transcriber

The four pictures at this table each show something that causes a change when added to ocean water.  Use your knowledge about the ocean to explain how these get introduced to the ocean water system and what happens when each one does.

1. How _____ gets into the ocean water system: _____

   _____

   What happens when _____ gets into the ocean water: _____

   _____

2. How _____ gets into the ocean water system: _____

   _____

   What happens when _____ gets into the ocean water: _____

   _____

3. How _____ gets into the ocean water system: _____

   _____

   What happens when _____ gets into the ocean water: _____

   _____

4. How _____ gets into the ocean water system: _____

   _____

   What happens when _____ gets into the ocean water: _____

   _____

Put your finished activity paper in the collection pocket on the side of the table at this station.

# Infer

Before beginning your investigation, write your group members' names by their jobs below.

_____Team Leader          _____Stenographer

_____Oceanographer        _____Transcriber

Look closely at the pictures of ocean resources at this table.  Using your knowledge of the ocean's waters, match the resources to the area of the ocean in which they are found.  Write the names of the resources in the correct spaces on the ocean diagram below.

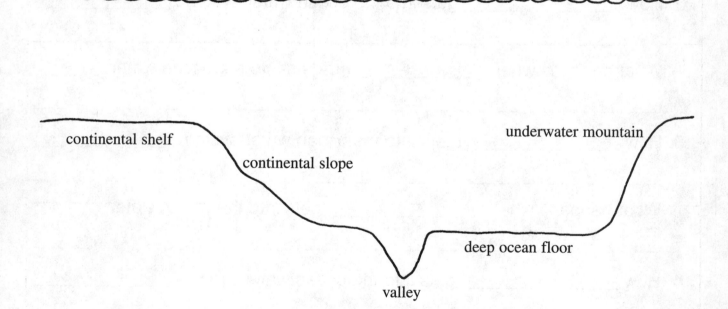

Put your finished activity paper in the collection pocket on the side of the table at this station.

# Apply

Before beginning your investigation, write your group members' names by their jobs below.

_____Team Leader          _____Stenographer

_____Oceanographer          _____Transcriber

At this station you will find a ball of clay, a piece of aluminum foil, a sheet of paper, and 15 paper clips. From each of those three materials, make a shape that can float while carrying five paper clips. Draw a picture of the finished shapes in the spaces below.

| **Clay** |
| --- |
| |
| **Foil** |
| |
| **Paper** |
| |

Put your finished activity paper in the collection pocket on the side of the table at this station.

# Science Safety

Discuss the necessity for science safety rules. Reinforce the rules on this page or adapt them to meet the needs of your classroom. You may wish to reproduce the rules for each student or post them in the classroom.

1. Begin science activities only after all directions have been given.

2. Never put anything in your mouth unless it is required by the science experience.

3. Always wear safety goggles when participating in any lab experience.

4. Dispose of waste and recyclables in proper containers.

5. Follow classroom rules of behavior while participating In science experiences.

6. Review your basic class safety rules every time you conduct a science experience.

## You can still have fun and be safe at the same time!

# My Ocean Journal

Ocean journals are an effective way to integrate science and language arts. Students are to record their observations, thoughts, and questions about past science experiences in a journal to be kept in the science area. The observations may be recorded in sentences or sketches which keep track of changes both in the science item or in the thoughts and discussions of the students.

Ocean journal entries can be completed as a team effort or an individual activity. Be sure to model the making and recording of observations several times when introducing the journals to the science area.

Use the student recordings in the ocean journals as a focus for class science discussions. You should lead these discussions and guide students with probing questions, but it is usually not necessary for you to give any explanation. Students come to accurate conclusions as a result of classmates' comments and your questioning. Ocean journals can also become part of the students' portfolios and overall assessment program. Journals are valuable assessment tools for parent and student conferences as well.

## How to Make an Ocean Journal

1. Cut two pieces of 8.5" x 11" (22 cm x 28 cm) construction paper to create a cover. Reproduce page 88 and glue it to the front cover of the journal. Allow students to draw ocean pictures in the box on the cover.
2. Insert several ocean journal pages. (See page 89.)
3. Staple together and cover stapled edge with book tape.

# My
# Ocean
# Journal

**Name** _____

# My Ocean Journal

This is what happened: _____

_____

_____

_____

This is what I learned: _____

_____

_____

_____

# Assessment Forms

The following form may be used as part of the assessment process for hands-on science experiences.

## Science Anecdotal Record Form

Date:_____

Scientist's Name: _____

Topic: _____

Assessment Situation: _____

Instructional Task: _____

Behavior/Skill Observed: _____

_____

_____

_____

_____

This behavior/skill is important because: _____

_____

_____

_____

_____

# Assessment Forms *(cont.)*

The evaluation form below provides student groups with the opportunity to evaluate the group's overall success.

## Cooperative Group Evaluation

Assignment: _____

Date: _____

| Scientists | Jobs |
|---|---|
| _____ | _____ |
| _____ | _____ |
| _____ | _____ |
| _____ | _____ |

As a group, decide which face you should fill in and complete the remaining sentences.

1. We finished our assignment on time, and we did a good job.
2. We encouraged each other, and we cooperated with each other.

3. We did best at _____

_____

4. Next time we could improve at_____

_____

# Oceanographer Award

## This is to certify that

_____
*Name*

## made a science discovery.

# *Congratulations!*

_____
*Teacher*

_____
*Date*

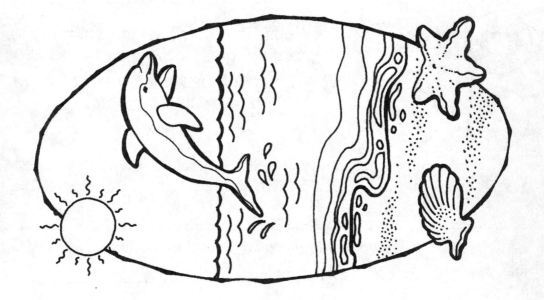

# Glossary

**C**

**continental shelf**—a shallow underwater plain that is the edge of a continent.

**continental slope**—the slope between the continental shelf and the floor of the deep ocean.

**coral reef**—mass of living coral animals attached to a wall of millions of dead coral polyp skeletons.

**crest**—the top of a wave.

**current**—the movement of water through the ocean.

**D**

**dehydrate**—to remove water.

**E**

**ebb tide**—when the water moves away from the shore.

**experiment**—a means of proving or disproving an hypothesis.

**F**

**fresh water**—water in rivers or streams; it is not salty.

**G**

**gravity**—the force that pulls objects toward the center of the Earth.

**H**

**hydrologic cycle**—the process in which the earth's water evaporates, falls to Earth as rain or snow, returns to the sea in rivers, and is then evaporated again.

**I**

**iceberg**—chunks of ice which break off the ends of glaciers and float in the sea.

**Indian Ocean**—the ocean which lies east of Africa and is smaller than either the Pacific or the Atlantic Oceans.

**investigation**—to observe something and then perform a systematic inquiry in order to answer what was originally observed.

**O**

**observation**—to notice or look at something.

**ocean**—the body of salt water that covers 70% of the Earth's surface.

**oceanography**—the scientific study of the ocean.

**P**

**Pacific Ocean**—the largest and deepest of the oceans.

**pollutant**—something that makes the water, air, or soil unclean.

**procedure**—the series of steps that is carried out when doing an experiment.

**purification**—the process through which water is made clean for drinking and public use.

**Q**

**question**—a formal way of inquiring about a particular topic.

# Glossary *(cont.)*

**R**

**results**—the data collected after performing an experiment.

**S**

**scientific method**—the systematic process of proving or disproving a given question, following an observation.

**scientific process skills**—the skills necessary to have in order to be able to think critically.

**sea**—a large body of salty water that is smaller than an ocean.

**shore**—where the surface of the ocean touches the land.

**sonar**—a system of detecting objects in water; the abbreviation for sound navigation ranging.

**T**

**tide**—a change in the ocean's water level caused by the pull of the moon and sun on the Earth.

**trade winds**—winds found north and south of the equator; they blow almost constantly toward the equator.

**trough**—the lowest point in a wave between two crests.

**tsunami**—huge, fast-moving wave triggered by an earthquake or an underground volcano.

**V**

**variable**—the changing factor of an experiment.

**vent**—an opening in the ocean floor; a vent is formed when ocean water seeps into cracks in the ocean floor.

**W**

**wavelength**—the distance between the crests of waves.

# Bibliography

Arnold, Caroline. *Bodies of Water.* Franklin Watts, 1985.

Bendick, Jeanne. *Exploring an Ocean Tide Pool.* Henry Holt & Co., 1992.

Bramwell, Martyn. *Oceanography.* Hampstead, 1989.

Cecil, Laura (compiled by). *A Thousand Yards of Sea.* Greenwillow Books, 1992. (Stories and poems about the ocean.)

Cole, Joanna. *The Magic School Bus on the Ocean Floor.* Scholastic, 1992.

Cole, Sheila. *When the Tide Is Low.* Lothrop, Lee, and Shepard, 1985.

Daegling, Mary. *Monster Seaweeds: The Story of the Giant Kelps.* Macmillan, 1987.

Davies, Eryl. *Ocean Frontiers.* Viking Press, 1980.

DeBeauregard, Diane, C. *The Blue Planet: Seas & Oceans.* Young Discovery Library, 1989.

Epstein, Sam and Beryl Epstein. *What's for Lunch? The Eating Habits of Seashore Creatures.* Macmillan, 1985.

Gibbons, Gail. *Sunken Treasure.* Harper Collins, 1988.

Gibbs, B. *Ocean Facts.* Usborne, 1991.

Goldin, Augusta. *The Bottom of the Sea.* Harper Collins, 1966.

Heinrichs, Susan. *The Atlantic Ocean, The Indian Ocean, and The Pacific Ocean.* Childrens Press, 1986.

Heller, Ruth. *How to Hide An Octopus and Other Sea Creatures.* Putnam Publishing Group, 1992.

*Hidden Treasures of the Sea.* National Geographic Society, 1988.

Johnston, Tom. *Water, Water!* Gareth Stevens, 1985.

Kalman, Bobbie and Janine Schaub. *Wonderful Water.* Crabtree Publishing Company, 1992.

Kirkpatrick, Rena K. *Look at Shore Life.* Raintree Press, 1987.

Lambert, David. *The Oceans.* The Bookwright Press, 1984.

Lampton, Christopher. *Tidal Wave.* Millbrook Press, 1992.

Levine, Shar. *Projects for a Healthy Planet.* John Wiley & Sons, Inc., 1992.

*Life in the Water.* Time-Life, 1989.

Lye, Keith. *The Ocean Floor.* Franklin Watts, 1989.

Mariner, Tom. *Oceans.* Marshall Cavendish, 1990.

# Bibliography (cont.)

Marshak, Suzanna. *I Am the Ocean.* Arcade Publishing, 1991.

Matthews, Ruupert. *Record Breakers of the Sea.* Troll Associates, 1990.

McGovern, Ann and Eugenie Clark. *The Desert Beneath the Sea.* Scholastic, 1991.

Pearce, Q. L. *Tidal Waves & Other Ocean Wonders.* Julian Messner, 1989.

Pifer, Joanne. *EarthWise: Earth's Oceans.* WP Press, 1992.

Robinson, W. Wright. *Incredible Facts About the Ocean.* Dillon Press, Inc., 1990.

Rogers, Daniel. *Waves, Tides & Currents.* Franklin Watts, 1991.

Seixas, Judith S. *Water. What It Is, What It Does.* Greenwillow Books, 1987.

Seymour, Pete. *What's in the Deep Blue Sea?* Henry Holt and Company, 1990.

Silver, Donald M. *Seashore. One Small Square.* W.H. Freeman and Company, 1993.

Simon, Seymour. *How to Be an Ocean Scientist in Your Own Home.* J.B. Lippincott, 1988.

Stacy, Tom. *Earth, Sea & Sky.* Warwick Press, 1991.

Taylor, Barbara. *Rivers and Oceans.* Kingfisher Books, 1993.

Twist, Clint. *Seas & Oceans.* Macmillan, 1991.

Walpole, Brenda. *Water.* Warwick Press, 1987.

Wells, Susan. *The Illustrated World of Oceans.* Simon & Schuster, 1991.

Wood, Jenny. *Under the Sea.* Macmillan, 1991.

Yardley, Thompson. *Make a Splash! Care about the Ocean.* Millbrook Press, 1992.

## Technology

David C. Knight. *Let's Find Out About the Ocean.* Available from American School Publishers. 1-800-843-8855.

Knowledge Adventure. *UnderSea Adventure.* Available from Education Resources, 1-800-624-2926. Software.

The Learning Company. *Operation Neptune.* Available from Education Resources, 1-800-624-2926.

Orange Cherry. *20,000 Leagues Under the Sea.* Available from Education Resources, 1-800-624-2926. Software.

Software Toolworks. *Oceans Below.* Available from Education Resources, 1-800-624-2926.

*Tidepool Teaching Kit.* One-week units which include work sheets and classroom activities. Available ⌐ Sea Grant Education Program, Hatfield Marine Science Center, 2030 Marine Science Dr., ⌐ort, OR 97365. Phone 503-867-0271.